IDENTITY

STUDIES IN CRIME & PUNISHMENT

David A. Schultz and Christina DeJong
General Editors

Vol. 13

PETER LANG
New York • Washington, D.C./Baltimore • Bern
Frankfurt am Main • Berlin • Brussels • Vienna • Oxford

David A. May
and James E. Headley

IDENTITY
THEFT

PETER LANG
New York • Washington, D.C./Baltimore • Bern
Frankfurt am Main • Berlin • Brussels • Vienna • Oxford

Library of Congress Cataloging-in-Publication Data
May, David A.
Identity theft / David A. May and James E. Headley.
p. cm. — (Studies in crime and punishment; vol. 13)
Includes bibliographical references.
1. False personation—United States. 2. False personation—United States—
Prevention. I. Headley, James E. II. Title. III. Series.
HV6679 .M28   364.16'3—dc21   2002072870
ISBN 0-8204-5844-9
ISSN 1529-2444

Bibliographic information published by **Die Deutsche Bibliothek**.
Die Deutsche Bibliothek lists this publication in the "Deutsche
Nationalbibliografie"; detailed bibliographic data is available
on the Internet at http://dnb.ddb.de/.

Cover design by Joni Holst

The paper in this book meets the guidelines for permanence and durability
of the Committee on Production Guidelines for Book Longevity
of the Council of Library Resources.

*David May would like to dedicate this book to Emily.
I hope that her identity will always be as unique
as her personality.*

*James Headley would like to dedicate this book
to his parents, Carl and Margaret.*

Contents

Acknowledgments

The authors would like to acknowledge the assistance of Sean Jackson and Matt Zuchetto.

Foreword

Identity Theft delivers clear, illuminating descriptions of identity theft and its causes while at the same time comprehensively compiling and describing the current state of the law and policy challenges in the field of identity theft.

This book details an impressive array of statistical data that is strong but does not neglect the personal stories of individual humans suffering incredibly personal and human losses from identity theft. In writing a book that manages the delicate balance between "the forest and the trees," between the losses identity theft inflicts upon the individual and greater society, May and Headley have managed to create a scholarly, comprehensive work that is still grounded in personally identifiable experiences.

At the "forest" level, this book serves as a comprehensive resource for data and developments on the financial and legal impacts of identity theft. In analyzing legislative responses and government agency enforcement, it accomplishes the significant task of collecting and identifying information from often fledgling or brand new government and private sector efforts. In comparing and making sense of the data on financial and other losses suffered by businesses and, most importantly, victims, it consistently identifies and interprets the meaning and significance behind what is often a glut of raw numbers. Importantly, this book addresses these issues with an eye to the wider and less intuitive impacts on society, such as the compelling connection between identity theft and organized crime, international terrorism, and immigration issues.

At the "trees" level, May and Headley again do a compelling job of showing the important personal losses that underlie this crime and make it so significant and damaging to its victims. In clear and concise writing that sacrifices no granularity but is still approachable, May and Headley write a reference manual, policy report, law update, victim's tool, and thought-provoking reading all at once. With a keen eye to the technological advances that have both caused, and may help solve, this crisis, May and Headley find the specifics. Through case studies and detailed recounting of the personal stories of actual identity theft victims, the damage identity theft wreaks is made clear. Ultimately, the scholastic and non-anecdotal retelling of these different stories makes the argument that identity theft deserves significant, immediate attention and an effective response even more compelling. In my experience working with consumer advocates in the legislative effort to provide victims of identity theft with real tools to recover their losses and reclaim their identity, I have heard personally several of the stories retold within. It is rewarding to know that serious academic and scholastic attention is being brought to bear on the real, and in some cases easily solvable, problems faced by far too many Americans. I not only commend reading this book, but would also urge the reader to actively support the real and necessary reforms that will help solve this epidemic.

Senator Maria Cantwell
Washington, DC
February 2003

1. Financial impact < business victims
2. Consequences
3. Prevention

Introduction

Identity theft is certainly not a new crime. The idea of assuming the identity of another for some purpose or other is
as old as the idea of identity itself. Many figures have "acquired" new identities, from famous outlaws of the Old
West to tragic figures in Shakespearean plays. The idea
may not be new but the scope of identity theft in recent
years, as a crime of significant social and economic consequences, is a wholly new phenomenon, and one that has
increased dramatically in frequency and severity since the
early 1990s. In its most basic sense, identity theft is a simple matter. It can be defined most simply as the obtaining
and fraudulent use of the individual identifying information of another person. The simplicity of such a definition
certainly hides much of the complexity of the real problems

that exist. Identity theft can, for instance, take the form of simple and often relatively innocuous activities, such as using false identification to gain access to some restricted area, like a bar or even an 'R' rated movie. It can be as simple as using another person's name to subscribe to magazines or join a CD club.

If these types of theft of identity were all that occurred, most people would probably view identity theft as more of an inconvenience than a crime. Having to track down a roommate to retrieve a driver's license or dealing with the mailings from the CD club may be a bother but it is seldom a truly significant disruption. Far too often, however, the initially simple idea of the fraudulent use of the identity of another is much more serious and has consequences and implications that are much more severe. Identity theft can have enormous impacts on individuals, on families, and ultimately on society as a whole. It is a crime that can also be used to facilitate larger criminal enterprises. Identity theft has been linked to some of the largest scourges of American society, such as terrorism or drug smuggling. As part of that larger pattern of crime, it can be both a catalyst and a result. Criminals can use it to perpetrate crimes or to hide from detection, prosecution, and punishment. Most often, however, identity theft is undertaken for one basic purpose—real and frequently significant financial gain.

A talented criminal can take another individual's Social Security number, credit card, checking, or other personal identifying information and use those records to impersonate the individual. Manipulating a system that is increasingly reliant on nonpersonal identifiers to define individual identity, a motivated criminal can take very small amounts of information and, at least for a short time, convince the system that he or she is someone else entirely. Using their newly stolen and assumed identity, these criminals can drain bank accounts and obtain fraudulent credit, amassing enormous debts very quickly in the name of someone else. In the process, these thieves are destroying credit, reputations, and a carefully built sense and reality of financial and individual security.

As we shall see, however, that type of significant and frequently short-term financial gain may not necessarily be the motive in every instance of identity theft. Hiding in the anonymity that comes from assuming the identity of another, the worst of these thieves can commit crimes with impunity; their true self has much less fear of being caught and punished, or they may use their assumed identity to effectively hide from law enforcement after those crimes.

Perhaps the most insidious form of this new type of crime involves the theft not of money but of the most valuable asset we each possess, our true private identity. Using a few simple pieces of information and even more readily available tools, it is possible for identity thieves to take the basics of individual identity and assume those, creating what in essence amounts to a duplicate person. The objective in this crime is not the "quick score" of money but rather the long-term value offered by having the identity of another. It is easy to imagine many reasons why someone would want to disappear as her true self and reappear as someone else. Perhaps there is some element in her real past that makes a new start seem worth the risks. This type of thief, if she is careful and skillful, can live and work for years or even decades as this duplicate person. She can often hold jobs, raise a family and even send her kids to school, all from within a stolen and assumed identity. Chapter 1 provides a brief look at the problems of identity in the modern world and the several different types and degrees of identity theft, from the small and relatively innocuous to those that have destroyed credit ratings, families, and lives.

Because it is a complex crime with many facets, identity theft can be hard for the criminal justice system to even track. While reliable statistics about the prevalence and cost of identity theft are hard to come by, it is clear that it is a significant problem and that the problem is growing at an alarming rate. Almost every statistic available shows an increase in the frequency of identity theft and an increase in the reporting of that theft as a crime. Often those numbers show a doubling or even tripling from only a few years ago. The lowest estimates suggest half a million incidents a year in the United States alone. As with most other types of crime, the actual number of incidents of identity theft is probably much higher, perhaps as much as two or even three times the reported rate. By far the most reported category of identity theft crime involves credit card fraud. The increasing frequency of identity theft, as significant as it may be, is itself outpaced by the rising costs. Credit card companies alone estimate their year 2000 losses from identity theft at over one billion dollars. Chapter 2 examines some trends in identity theft by looking at the best available data on how often it occurs, who has responsibility for stemming the tide, and how much the crimes and the societal response are actually costing the system as a whole.

Identity theft can indeed be viewed as a simple matter, but a closer look reveals that even the term itself is actually far too simple for what is really going on. Expressed in the singular, the term often hides the complexity of a multitude of crimes involved. Below its surface, the term *identity theft* subsumes a multitude of different types of criminal activity: bank fraud, credit card fraud, securities fraud, and many others. Deeper still, those criminal activities are themselves often part of a larger story of crime and criminal activity of which they often play only a small part. Identity theft may be simply a precursor to a much larger crime spree or it may be a means of escaping punishment once those crimes have been committed. It can be difficult to even determine whether to charge identity theft as a separate crime. The underlying charge is often expressed as fraud or theft, terms that help to hide the enormity and the complexity of the problem from the public and from the system that is or at least should be trying to correct the problem.

Many of the crimes perpetrated with identity theft as a component are what are often called high-tech crimes or

white-collar crimes. If an identity thief requires personal information about his victim, the growth of technology plays
right into his hands. The advent and rapid expansion of the
Internet and the desire of the public for easier and faster online shopping, online banking, online chat, and online living
has proven to be an enormous benefit to those searching
for new ways to break the law and maybe the bank. Our society has started to take private information too much for
granted. Many crucial bits of information that we type into
our computers, transmit over the phone by voice or fax, or
write down every day with hardly a second thought define
who we are in a system that is becoming increasingly complex. With just a few crucial pieces of this host of information, a seasoned identity thief can steal your identity and
your life in very short order, often without ever seeing you
or interacting with you personally at all. The thief who
steals your identity and does perhaps irreparable harm to
your life may not even have to be in the same country as
you, let alone the same city. The rise of a largely electronic
society has done nothing to hinder and much to help the
cause of the would-be identity thief.

While a boon for those searching for ways to use this
glut of available information and the ease of access to
make a fast and illegal buck or for other nefarious purposes, the rapid technological developments of the last half
of the twentieth century have presented enormous challenges to the criminal justice system. In many ways, the
identity theft that is occurring today is unlike any other
crime. It is a new breed of crime, for a new type of criminal. Chapter 3 looks at some of the challenges that the information age and the rising tide of the technology revolu-
tion have created for law enforcement as well as for legal
and criminal justice systems.

All of this has left the system and legal practitioners at all
levels often struggling to play catch-up in a system of outdated laws and frequently outdated thinking. Chapter 4
considers the specific federal statutory implications and
looks at how statutory enactments in recent years have

tried to stem if not reverse the tide of identity theft. Inroads are being made as loopholes in the existing laws are closed or restricted, but the problem does not seem to be diminishing overall. Certainly any real attempt to stem the flood of identity theft requires a concerted effort involving both the federal and state governments working in concert.

States were slower than the federal system to react to identity theft as a crime. In recent years, however, states have taken the lead in important ways in fighting this crime. Chapter 5 examines the responses and innovations of several selected states. It is helpful to examine how the most proactive states deal with identity theft. These state efforts can act as leaders for other states and perhaps even provide a model for national identity theft laws. Within states, state constitutional law, case law, and statutory enactments are all important and applicable to identity theft law and enforcement. California, Florida, Illinois, and Washington all provide good examples of the scope of the identity theft problem and how that problem can be dealt with by law enforcement. In fact, California, Florida, and Illinois represent three of the five states most impacted by identity theft. The statute enacted in Washington State is perhaps the most comprehensive in the nation, as Washington has been a consistent leader in attempting to define and enact new responses to the problem. Case studies looking at how some statutes are applied and how some cases are handled are examined in chapter 6.

Determining the scope of the problem is really only the first tentative step toward combating and resolving it. The recent rise of identity theft as a new and important crime type, the highly complex and technological nature of some of the crimes, and simple logistical issues such as jurisdictional overlap have all served to frustrate enforcement of even those laws that are on the books. The federal government and the states both have significant responsibility for combating identity theft crime. Specifically, the federal government gave the duty of attacking identity theft to the Federal Trade Commission and the Department of Justice.

States and the federal government are struggling hard to come to grips with this rapidly expanding problem. Law enforcement and the legal profession are trying to find ways to combat a crime that often occurs with incredible rapidity and often at great distance. There may indeed be ways to slow down the growth of identity theft if we are willing to take the steps necessary.

CHAPTER 1

Problems of Identity and Identity Thieves

Problems of Identity

We would all like to think of ourselves as unique individuals. But defining that individuality can be a difficult proposition. We believe that there is something inherent in a person that makes him or her different from everyone else. These differences can be something tangible or even easily visible, like fingerprints. For the purposes of defining identity, there are few traits that are as sure as the human fingerprint. While it is possible for two individuals to have the exact same set of prints, the likelihood is so small as to be statistically insignificant. Fingerprints, then, seem to provide some basis for an argument of individuality or individual identity.

Other factors, like the features of a face or the sound of a voice, all provide distinction for us among what we believe and perceive to be unique persons. The differences can also be intangible. Philosophy and religion have debated from the beginning of time the uniqueness of each human soul, the distinct qualities of intellect, or the divine fire, things unseen that make each of us unique. Utilizing the tangible and perhaps even the intangible, we can all recognize hundreds or even thousands of unique individuals in our lives.[1] We know, even if unconsciously, that we as well as all of those around us are unique, different from each other, and they are all different from us.

What is provided above is merely an approximation of what constitutes our individual identity. On the one hand, identifiers like fingerprints belie entirely the abstract nature of identity as a great intangible. While important for philosophy or religion, such abstractions are of little interest to a thief of identity and consequently for this discussion.[2] This thief does not have to *be* someone else in any abstract sense; he or she has only *to appear to be* someone else. Even then, that appearance can, in many instances, be only a crude approximation of the actual individual. On the other hand, the description above fails to address the complexities of even these simple identifying characteristics, the day-to-day realities of defining and maintaining individual identity in the modern world. Individual fingerprints or the patterns of blood vessels in the retina of the human eye are nearly perfect identifiers. Like DNA or other complex identifiers, they are nearly impossible to fake and are almost completely unique to a single individual. Their complexity, exactly the trait that makes them so valuable, unfortunately means that they are simply too cumbersome to utilize effectively. The usual frequency of identification required by our society mandates that identification be accomplished quickly and efficiently, without recourse to complex and expensive DNA testing or even fingerprint analysis.[3]

The difficulty in easily utilizing the best individual identifiers leads to the beginnings of the problem in protecting identity and the opening of a window of opportunity for would-be thieves of identity. Unable to utilize the truly unique and relatively nonreplicable factors that define our physical individuality, we are forced, for the sake of convenience, to use less secure means of determining identity. The means most commonly used are factors known as base identifiers. Far from being unique to a single individual, each of these base identifiers is shared by large numbers of individuals. Some are relatively complex and therefore difficult to replicate, but others are simple to change or assume. These base identifiers could include the full name of an individual, his or her birth date, age, race or ethnicity, sex, hair color, or height. While not unique to a single individual, a quality base identifier will hopefully at least remain consistent over the life of an individual. Shared by many individuals, most single base identifiers have little value in maintaining or verifying a unique identity. When used in combination, however, these base identifiers can start to do a reasonably effective job of defining a single individual as unique.

The most common base identifier is the full name of an individual. Many of us believe our names to be different, special, a great personal identifier. It is surprising to many to see the results of an Internet search of their full name; even a name that is relatively uncommon will probably turn up dozens if not thousands of people with exactly the same name as yours. So, a full name by itself is not a terribly useful base identifier. That usefulness is lessened even further given the fact that names, unlike DNA or fingerprints, can be changed with relative ease. Including a second base identifier yields substantially narrowed results. Doing the same full-name search again but this time restricted to those individuals who share the birth date or even birth year yields significantly fewer matches. The inclusion of each additional base identifier narrows the number of matches even further. The more specific the identifier added, the more the results are narrowed. A sufficient number of base identifiers of sufficient quality will, in all likelihood, produce only a single result. How many identifi-

ers are needed and which are the most effective in discrim-
inating among individuals depend greatly on several factors. The most important of these factors is the size of the
pool of possible matches. If the pool of possible matches is
small enough or, conversely, if it is not too large, a few simple base identifiers used in combination is probably sufficient to keep you or any individual separated from everyone else in the pool. So, for most systems, a combination
of these base characteristics is sufficient security, or at least
most systems treat it as such. Your full name, your birth
date, and a picture to provide physical identifiers provide
enough differentiation between you and others for most
systems to function quite well. Even systems that we expect to be very secure rely on these base identifiers.
Driver's licenses, student ID cards, and even U.S. passports
rely on these base characteristics as the primary means of
identifying you as you.

In the twenty-first century, the possibility that the potential matches mentioned above will remain a small pool is an
increasingly unlikely event. As the population of possible
matches increases rapidly, the likelihood that some other
single individual will carry the same critical set of base identifiers increases as well. At some point, when the pool becomes large enough, the likelihood that you are not
uniquely identifiable on the basis of those factors alone has
to be faced as a real possibility. Fortunately, there is an easy
and effective short-term solution. That solution involves the
addition of man-made identifiers. These created identifiers
come most often in the form of numerical ID numbers. If
each individual has a unique numerical identifier to supplement the inherent base identifiers, then regardless of the
size of the pool, each individual can be discriminated. In the
United States the most common and by far the most important numerical identifier of this type has become the individual Social Security number. While many other identifiers,
such as driver's license numbers or student ID numbers,
have been appended to most of our lives, we shall see in a
moment that many if not all are traceable in fact to our first

numerical identifier, the Social Security number. While offering the promise of an easy solution to a problem, the use of numerical or other man-made identifiers also widens the window of opportunity used by thieves.

The Social Security number was never intended to be a widely used identifier of individuals. The Social Security Act of 1935 created a system of individual Social Security numbers to be used only by the Social Security program, linking an individual and his or her contributions with a specific account. Beginning in 1943,[4] however, the usefulness of a single and unique numerical identifier began to be clear, and the mandated uses for this unique personal identifier began to mount. In that year, President Roosevelt signed an executive order that required federal agencies to use the number when creating any new record-keeping systems and to provide these Social Security numbers to everyone in the United States. In 1961 the Internal Revenue Service (IRS) began to use it as a taxpayer ID number. With the link established between the number and the larger individual, many new public and private requests for its use began to appear. The Tax Reform Act of 1976[5] gave authority to many state agencies to use the number in order to establish identities.

At the federal level, this means that most programs, from food stamps to federal crop insurance payments, are tracked on the basis of the nine-digit Social Security number. Today, tax, welfare, driver's license, and motor vehicle registration authorities in many states rely on a Social Security number for record keeping and to establish identity. Local governments also use this unique identifier for tax records, property ownership, traffic ticket records, and a host of other documentation. Even many private organizations have until recently continued to use the Social Security number as the sole unique identifier, and information on individual Social Security numbers has become readily available and widely circulated.

There have been attempts to limit the use of Social Security numbers as identifiers, such as the Privacy Act of 1974 as

updated in 2000,[6] which requires specific statutory authority before any agency can request the Social Security number of an individual for tracking or record keeping. Difficult
to enforce and lacking any real penalties, the 1974 Privacy
Act has been largely ignored by those requesting the information as well as by those providing it. Few of us even
pause to consider the implications of filling out the box that
requests that seemingly innocuous piece of information for
almost anyone who asks. We routinely provide that crucial
identifier to insurance companies, credit card companies,
health care providers, college registrars, prospective employers, and even department store clerks who ask politely.
None of these uses are codified in law and certainly none
are required.

While we have become relatively blasé and accepting of
the idea that a social security number is, de facto, a national
identification number, identity thieves certainly have not.
The unique number, because of its widespread use in
non–Social Security applications, means that this single
piece of information can provide a thief with access to vast
amounts of information and, in our society, represents a
linchpin in advancing identity theft. Knowing only a name
and utilizing easily available Social Security number databases, a professional identity thief can have access to information that most people think to be very secure. No records
tied to that single number, from financial records to college
transcripts to telephone bills, are secure. In fact, nationwide,
as much as 81 percent of Social Security number misuse
may be related to identity theft.[7] Of course, not all misuses
of a Social Security number, even in cases of identity theft
are equal in scope or magnitude.

Given a name and that single piece of information, a determined identity thief can acquire all of the information
necessary to "become" that person. A credit history provides a wealth of supposed private information, including
credit card and bank account numbers and balances. Tax
and voting records reveal addresses past and present as
well as a host of information about your private financial

dealings, cars owned, names of spouses, maiden names, past addresses, employment history, divorces, legal judgments, names and information on other relatives and friends who have served as references, and even unpublished telephone numbers.

The exponential growth in record keeping in the twentieth century, coupled with an almost equally rapid rise in population, has made questions of identity much more difficult. We no longer necessarily know personally all or even a majority of the people with whom we interact, and they do not know us. We have become a nation that relies on base and man-made identifiers to safeguard identity. It should be obvious that this type of system promotes almost as many problems as it addresses. The more linked these records become,[8] particularly under the umbrella of a single numerical identifier, the easier and more likely it is that any individual can and will be the victim of an identity thief.

While any violation of the identity of an individual is a serious matter, the degrees of theft and levels of destruction that can be wrought vary enormously. The degree of devastation that an individual experiences can depend on several factors including how quickly he realizes that an identity thief has him targeted or whether the thief who has stolen his identity is acting alone or is part of a larger organized operation. The next sections examine various types of identity thieves and their goals.

The Individual Identity Thief

Identity theft can be and in fact frequently is a basically innocuous and perhaps even unnoticed intrusion by a roommate.[9] It can also be a life-altering and financially apocalyptic crime of international intrigue. A single individual can undertake the crime acting alone, or a cabal of people separated even by enormous distances but working in collusion can undertake it. The effect as well as the real costs, monetary and otherwise, can be vastly different. In general, identity thieves can be broken down into these two main categories—those acting alone and those acting in concert with others. Taken together, these thieves are responsible for as many as 500,000 identity thefts per year, or 1 every 30 seconds in the United States. Of course, there are differences in type within these large groups.

Once a thief has stolen an identity, he can use it to accomplish many other crimes including credit card fraud or bank fraud. Often, a thief will use a stolen identity to commit multiple crimes across a wide range of criminal enterprises and 22% of reports of identity theft indicate more than one category. The uses to which stolen information is most often put are summarized in Table 1.

Many thieves of identity acting alone have a decidedly low-tech approach to gathering the personal information required to commit their crimes. As with the majority of thieves, most individual identity thieves operate in a hit-and-run fashion. Whether first-time thief or long-term professional, these individuals are looking primarily for a quick boost in income, a fast score, and a clean escape. An easy and relatively low risk option is to steal identity and money from someone else. As discussed above, the Social Security number can provide nearly instant access to a host of information on a person. To access that crucial piece of information, many individual identity thieves will engage in common street crime such as purse snatching or mugging. The less bold may just as frequently take the nonviolent approach of sorting through garbage cans full of discarded credit card offers and bank statements. They are well aware that many of these types of documents that we throw away intact contain crucial identifiers that he or she can use to work backwards to the all-important Social Security number. Even eavesdropping on conversations taking place on public phones can gather the thief information whose value we do not consider when it is requested, but he or she certainly does.

The thief concerned only with the shortest-term benefit may not need anything more than a quick sift through a garbage can. Finding a credit card offer in the trash or stealing

TABLE 1

Information Misuse	Frequency
Credit Card Fraud	42%
Phone or Utility Fraud	22%
Bank Fraud	17%
Employment Fraud	9%
Government or Benefits Fraud	8%
Loan Fraud	6%
Attempted Identity Theft	8%
Other Fraud	16%

The data come from the Sentinel database information in the 2003 FTC report on fraud and identity theft and are based on 161,819 victim reports.

outgoing mail from a mailbox and, if necessary, using a change of address form, this thief can use an existing credit card number or quickly establish a new credit account, run up sizeable debt on it, and disappear before the victim even realizes that a new account has been established or that any fraud has taken place. In the highly linked and technologically dependent society of the new millennium, almost any piece of information is sufficient to start the hunt. Even a business card, usually freely given, contains a wealth of information that can start a committed identity thief down the path to stealing identity and ultimately large sums of money.

Not all individual thieves resort to this street-level approach to their crime. Some, better financed and more sophisticated, utilize technology to their advantage. A recent scam revealed by the Federal Trade Commission involved the sending of fake emails to people. In these emails, individuals were informed that their Internet service account would be terminated unless they updated their account information and supplied a new valid credit card number, with expiration date. The email asked them to respond with the credit information, and their Social Security number for "verification," as well as their sign-in name and password. Given that wealth of supposedly private identifying information, a thief can, in a matter of hours, run up enormous debt. It might seem obvious that no reputable business would ask for such sensitive information to be transmitted over nonencrypted email. What is painfully obvious to some, however, is not so clear to others, and many have been victimized by this and similar identity theft scams.

One other type of individual acting alone should be mentioned as well. Different than the others, this thief is less concerned with financial gain in the usual sense. He or she is interested in the possibility of assuming the identity of another person for the long term. These individuals, while less damaging initially, have the potential to produce colossal long-term harm. The long-term identity thief is not interested in the quick and easy cash that attracts most thieves. He or she is interested in the identity of another for its own sake. This thief wants to become a second you, starting a whole new and separate life utilizing your name, Social Security number, and whatever other identifiers are necessary. These long-term thieves can live for years or even decades as another person. Because they are not interested in the financial rewards of their theft, they frequently pay the bills they amass, hold jobs, and even raise families.

The most common reason for assuming the identity of another in the long term is obviously to escape from a negative past. Unpaid child support, bad credit or debts, failed attempts at education, even divorces and bankruptcies all disappear with the creation and assumption of a new identity. Someone wishing to lose his or her past could certainly start over again without stealing an identity. He or she could create a brand new identity with careful planning. It is easier, however, to assume an identity that already exists, and the benefits to the thief are enormous. He or she does not have to establish a credit history; the victim has already done that. The thief does not have to fake college transcripts or an employment history because the victim already has those. Every bad thing that the thief has done in his or her life is replaced by all of the good things in the life of the victim. Assuming the life of another, the thief can have everything she wants and can have it almost instantly.

Assuming that the thief does things correctly and carefully, she is nearly impossible to catch. These thieves are usually tripped up when they actually pay their federal income taxes. The Social Security number, which doubles as the taxpayer ID number, appearing on two forms—those of the victim and those of the thief—raises immediate red flags for the IRS. There are, of course, ways around this problem for the seasoned thief. Incorporating himself and selling the services of a corporation avoids this potential trap. Because the corporation has its own tax identification number, the thief never has to report his own to the government.

Even more easily, a thief can obtain from the Internal Revenue Service an alternate taxpayer identification number that is different from his or her assumed Social Security number. This alternate number, known as an Individual Taxpayer Identification Number (ITIN) was created as a way to encourage illegal aliens and others in the United States who do not wish to obtain a Social Security number to pay their taxes. While certainly not its intent, this loophole in the law has been of significant benefit to many identity thieves.

The second most common failing of long-term assumption of the identity of another comes when these thieves apply for a U.S. passport. These fraudulent passports are frequently issued by the Department of State because, after all, the thief has all of the supporting documentation necessary to prove that he or she is that person. The problem comes when the real individual applies for a passport also, and again red flags are raised. Of course simply avoiding foreign travel or traveling only to countries in North America and the Caribbean that do not require a U.S. passport avoids this pitfall as well.

Certainly it is possible for these long-term thieves to cause enormous harm to the financial stability or reputation of an individual. Often those who have failed in a previous life will fail again in their second attempt. When the problems of their assumed identity become too large to handle, most of these thieves will simply jettison their stolen identity, relocate, and begin the process again. Even so, they may again run out on large debt, child support obligations, civil judgments, bankruptcies, or failed marriages. Because frequently they have been living with their assumed identity for a long period of time, they have had ample opportunity to create an enormous mess for the victim, a mess that in many ways is more difficult to untangle than the purely financial mess of the short-term thief.

As troubling and potentially devastating as this is, at least it is not the intent of the thief when he or she starts to build this alternate identity. A more sinister possibility exists. There is a small class of these long-term thieves who create and maintain alternate identities not to use on a daily basis but rather as cover when needed. The ability to 'be' someone else at a moment's notice allows these individuals to commit at least small-scale crimes with near impunity. If caught, they simply provide the police with an alternate, fictional, and ultimately stolen identity. Released on bail or bond, these miscreants disappear, never intending to appear to face the charges.[10]

For some unlucky individuals, the first time they learn that their identity has been stolen is when, having been pulled over for a routine traffic stop, they are arrested on an outstanding bench warrant issued in a state to which they have never been for a crime of which they have no knowledge. The time and energy to clear a name in these situations is daunting, with the onus and financial expenses of doing so being borne entirely by the victim of the crime. Perhaps most disturbing of all, however, is that for any one of us, there may be a duplicate living somewhere right now, unknown to us, using our most basic selves, our base and man-made identifiers, as his or her own.

Identity Theft as Big Business

Rings of identity theft have sprung up in recent years. While some of these groups are based in the United States, many more operate beyond its borders. Identity theft as big business has gone international. Large theft rings operate nationally and internationally by identifying a group to target, creating false identities in great quantity, and snatching as much cash as can be gathered in a short time. Often, within a matter of only a few days, these groups will have abandoned their newly created identities and relocated to a new area, either physically or virtually, on the lookout for the next community to attack.

The selection of a group to attack can seem almost random. Some theft rings target college students because this demographic usually has relatively unblemished credit records. Some choose with relative randomness from a geographic area, often to facilitate other parts of the fraud process. Many choose to target, for obvious reasons, members of high-income professions like physicians or lawyers and even celebrities. Others target groups of individuals who have personal information more readily available to the public, such as government employees or college professors. These crime rings have targeted many individuals who have unwittingly attracted the criminals' attention. Responding to online or postal mail "contests" or advertisements for cheap travel opportunities or even filling out questionnaires to get into a website can sometimes be an invitation to a thief to assume your identity.

After utilizing information brokers or even just information available on the Internet to cull out those with less than desirable credit or difficult to obtain Social Security numbers, the real process of deceit can begin. The process employed by these large rings is complex but highly efficient to its purpose—stealing as much as possible in as short a time as possible. Usually, the group establishes real addresses in the names of one or more of the intended victims as a place to have mail sent. Cheap apartments in large cities are usually selected for the ease with which they can be rented with minimal amounts of background checking. Additional addresses can be created through mail forwarding services and secretarial services or by renting post office boxes.

Opening new checking accounts in the names of the victims and using the newly created addresses is the first step in the fraud.

That first step is followed quickly by obtaining as many as nine lines of credit[11] per individual victim. Each of these new credit cards usually comes with "convenience checks," which can be used to write large amounts of cash out of the new credit line of one victim and into the fraudulent checking account of a second victim. From there, it can be withdrawn easily using the fake identification created in the name of the victims and spent however the thieves wish. Easily obtained retail credit lines are also established, frequently with a minimum of background checking, and used immediately to purchase big ticket items, particularly consumer electronics that are easily pawned, fenced, or privately sold. In the most extreme of these types of thefts, the ring may even buy automobiles using the credit of their victims or establish second mortgages on the homes of wealthy victims.

Once the credit lines are used to the limit, and before the creditors send the first bill, the group of thieves will quickly maximize its destructiveness by using the checking accounts that it has created to buy still more large ticket items, knowing that even if there is money in the account, it will be withdrawn long before the check is paid. After saturating an area with bad checks, but before they begin to be returned unpaid to merchants, the group simply walks away from all of the havoc it has created. The thieves collapse the entire operation. They will abandon the rented apartments with rent unpaid. They will leave behind phone and other services hooked-up and running but, again, unpaid. This group of thieves will simply disappear from the scene of their crimes to begin looking for the next group of victims to target.

Many of the individuals involved in these large rings never even enter the city or locality where the crimes take place. In fact, some may never even enter the United States at all. As chapter 3 explains in more detail, identity thieves are adept at using technology to their advantage. Many credit companies will still allow applications over the phone, some touting it as a wonderful point of convenience for consumers. Banks and other financial institutions are increasingly allowing online and phone access to set up, maintain, and transfer funds between accounts. Call forwarding services and mail redirection are easily and legally obtained throughout the United States. It is easily possible to carry on the appearance of life in one place while your physical self is hundreds or thousands of miles away. The advantage is obvious. While committing a whole series of crimes and defrauding many businesses and consumers, you remain far beyond the easy reach of local police even if your scheme does happen to come to light earlier than you expect.

Conclusion

The discussion above makes it seem that even a reasonably proficient identity thief would have an easy time stealing the identity of almost anyone in the United States. That is certainly the case. The scope of the problem of identity theft is enormous. As American society as well as the global society continues to grow, problems of identity become more pronounced. We can no longer live in a world where identification is a matter of personal recognition of one another. We cannot have real, personal knowledge of even a small fraction of the people who impact our daily lives and who are, in turn, impacted by many others. Once the personal, base identification becomes impractical or impossible, other means of defining identity must be created. Nonpersonal identifiers increasingly define identification and identity. These identifiers, precisely because they are random, lacking any meaningful connection to the individual, ironically have had the effect of making identity less rather than more secure. As we shall see, it may be possible to reverse this trend in the future through yet more technological advances. Whether it can be done in a practical way and quickly enough to thwart the next advances on the part of the thieves remains to be seen.

Unable for the moment to stop the tide of identity theft, we are left to pick up the pieces of the lives that are destroyed. As we will see in the next chapter, however, identity theft has enormous costs both in real dollars and in other, nonmonetary ways. Identity theft can and certainly does cost individuals millions of dollars each year. A victim of identity theft will spend an average of nearly 200 hours trying to clear his or her name and credit history. The monetary costs to avoid paying the fraudulent credit lines average nearly one thousand dollars and the process takes an average of nearly two years to complete. Above and beyond the cost to the individual victims, the costs to society of dealing with the deluge of new cases are growing rapidly. Federal and state governments as well as private companies are bearing that cost, which means that we are all bearing it monetarily and otherwise, through higher prices for goods and services and through diversion of tax monies away from other uses and toward this fight. Clearly, it is far preferable to avoid being a victim and for government to help in that effort than it is for either the individual or government to try and repair the damage after the fact.

CHAPTER 2

The Scope of the Problem

Prevalence

Estimating accurately the total number of identity theft occurrences in the United States on an annual basis is a nearly impossible task. The difficulty of arriving at quality estimates arises from several factors. First, as with many crimes, reported statistics from the government or private organizations all rely on reported incidences. Even assuming that the identity theft is noticed and that it is reported to law enforcement, it may not be categorized by local, state, or even federal law enforcement in such a way as to make it easily discernible as identity theft. It is possible that local police often incorrectly categorize identity theft as other

crimes such as forgery or credit card fraud. A second con-
founding factor is the lack of consistent definition of the
crime itself. Many agencies, including the Federal Bureau of
Investigation (FBI) do not view identity theft as a stand-
alone crime in most cases. Rather, it is viewed as only one
part of a larger pattern of criminal conduct. Finally, there is
the problem of multiple jurisdictions over the various components of identity theft at both the state and federal levels.
Several agencies at the federal level play distinct roles in the
tracking, investigation, and prosecution of identity theft. It
is not always the case that the data they collect and share fit
well or are consistent in type. Until some of these difficulties
are resolved, any estimates of the frequency and severity of
this crime may be, at best, a close guess.

There are then some real problems with trying to quan-
tify identity theft in the United States. That said, even relying solely on the reported incidence produces a picture that
is frightening enough. Estimates of the actual number of
victims of identity theft range from one-quarter to three-
quarters of a million people annually in the United States
alone. These estimates vary considerably; and generally,
the higher the estimate, the more emphasis must be placed
on the assumption that most if not all victims report the
crime.[1] Because of the difficulty in arriving at the actual
number of identity theft crimes annually, agencies such as
the FBI and the Federal Trade Commission (FTC) rely exten-
sively on proxy measures to estimate the prevalence of
identity theft. These proxy measures include the FTC database on identity theft, the number of fraud alerts posted to
credit agencies, and fraud reports to the Social Security Administration (SSA) through its fraud hotline.

The most common proxy measure is the FTC database
known as the Identity Theft Data Clearinghouse. The 1998
law that made identity theft a federal crime, the Identity
Theft and Assumption Deterrence Act, mandated that the
FTC "log and acknowledge the receipt of complaints by individuals who . . . have a reasonable belief that one or more
of their means of identification have been assumed, stolen

or otherwise unlawfully acquired."[2] The result of that mandate has been the creation by the FTC of a toll-free number for the collection of data and the dissemination of identity theft information to the public and to law enforcement agencies. At present, the database has a membership of 46 separate federal agencies, which both contribute to and draw from it.[3] The database is also accessed by more than 300 state agencies that have signed up to contribute and to have access through a secure web server known as Sentinel. As such, the database provides what is probably the best proxy measure of the real number of identity thefts that are taking place annually.

The number of complaints and the growth of that number are staggering. In 2000, the first full year of operation, the database collected and logged 31,000 consumer complaints about identity theft or identity fraud. By 2001, that number had jumped to 86,168, or a 277 percent increase in reported incidences. In the first five months of 2002, the database logged more than 55,000 complaints, or enough to put it on pace to reach more than 130,000 complaints in 2002.[4] In its first month of operation, the clearinghouse and database answered an average of 445 calls per week from citizens. By 2001 that average was over 2,000 per week, and during 2001 it was well over 3,000 per week. The volume of complaints about identity theft being logged by the FTC database makes it clear that whether the actual number is one-quarter or three-quarters of a million, the rate of identity theft is still increasing, apparently at an accelerated rate.

On January 22, 2003, the Federal Trade Commission released its annual report detailing consumer complaints about identity theft and listing the top ten fraud complaint categories reported by consumers. As in 2000 and 2001, identity theft topped the list of the complaints lodged in the FTC's Consumer Sentinel database. The total number of fraud complaints jumped from 220,000 in 2001 to 380,000 in 2002, and the dollar loss consumers attributed to the fraud they reported grew from $160 million in 2001 to $343 million in 2002. Of those complaints, almost 162,000 were complaints about identity theft, or 43 percent of the total. Of the more than 380 million reports received by the Sentinel database, 30 percent were related specifically to identity theft.[5]

As the number of cases reported to the database increases, the value of that database increases as well. As more and more state agencies as well as federal actors contribute to the database, the information becomes more detailed and comprehensive and more reliable. Quality information about crime and criminals is of paramount value to both criminal justice practitioners and scholars. Increasing levels of competent and reliable data can provide those seeking to understand identity theft with important demographic and statistical information that is not currently available. As important as that may be to scholars, the practical benefits of a reliable data source are even greater. As agencies at the state and federal levels begin to share information in meaningful ways, it is possible to do a much better job of proactive victim identification and matching perpetrators to specific crime patterns. Both of these possibilities can aid law enforcement and prosecutorial efforts, but the process of utilizing the database to its full potential is just beginning.[6]

The FTC database provides considerable information, but it may not, by itself, capture the entirety of the problem. Some victims of identity theft, assumption, or fraud may choose to deal with the problem on their own, without reporting it to law enforcement at all. A second and related indicator of identity theft may be the number of long-term fraud alerts that are placed on consumer credit files. These alerts, constituting a warning that someone may be using that account fraudulently, remain on the account for seven years, and provide long-term tracking data that are used primarily by the three major consumer reporting agencies in the United States. The General Accounting Office (GAO) reports that this type of fraud alert has increased substantially in recent years.[7] One of the three credit agencies reported fraud alert increases from 65,600 reports to 89,000,

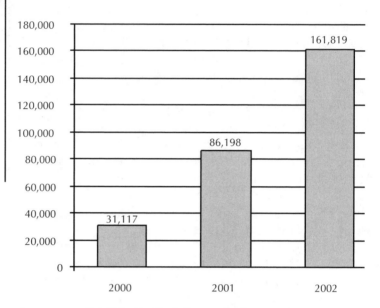

FIGURE 1. Total Identity Theft Reports by Year
Data represents total identity theft complaints to the Consumer Sentinel database.

between 1999 and 2000, an increase of 36 percent. A second of the three agencies reported that the number of complaints it received increased from 19,347 for the period
from July 1999 through June 2000 to more than 29,593 in
the same period one year later, an increase of more than 53
percent. These data are certainly not definitive and cannot
be viewed cumulatively as there is significant overlap in
consumer reports to the various agencies.[8] Nonetheless,
fraud alerts may support the notion that identity theft as a
crime is increasing in frequency.[9]

A final piece in the puzzle of identity theft statistics may
be the number of calls to the SSA fraud hotline. Precisely because the Social Security number is so valuable to thieves of
identity, this information can serve as a proxy measure for
the incidence of identity theft. As with the other measures,
the SSA has reported a substantial increase in the number
of reports to its hotline in recent years. The number of reported incidences of Social Security number misuse has in-

creased from about 11,000 in 1998 to more than 65,000 in 2001, a greater than fivefold increase.[10] If it is indeed accurate that more than 81 percent of those reported misuses involve identity theft or identity fraud, then again there is substantial support for recognizing that identity theft is an increasingly important component of the federal criminal justice picture. Increased emphasis on the crime in the media and continuing education, reporting, and tracking efforts[11] on the part of various government agencies probably contribute somewhat to an increased reporting of the crime.

These numbers paint quite a picture. However, even taken together, these proxy measures may not represent the universe of those affected by identity theft. If that is the case, then the problem and growth of this type of crime may be even more severe than suggested here. What we can say with certainty is that identity theft was the largest single type of fraud complaint received by the FTC in the past year. More than 42 percent of the fraud complaints received were related to identity theft. On the list of the top ten types of complaints received, identity theft alone was responsible for a higher percentage than the next seven categories combined.[12]

Federal Actors

The scope of the problem and the multiplicity of actors in the federal-level identity theft arena is daunting by law enforcement standards and certainly adds to the difficulty when talking about identity theft statistics. At the federal level there are five main nonjudicial actors that have a law enforcement role in deterring or prosecuting identity theft: the FTC, The SSA, The Department of Justice, the Department of the Treasury, and the Postal Inspection Service all have significant jurisdiction or statutory mandate in this area.

The FTC has a broad statutory mandate to act as a national consumer protection agency. It is authorized under the Federal Trade Commission Act (15 USC § 45[a]) to take action against "unfair or deceptive acts or practices" and is granted the authority to bring civil actions in federal district court or to utilize bureaucratic and administrative channels available to it. The FTC is also responsible for more than 45 additional statutes dealing with almost every conceivable area of trade and commerce, from the Fair Credit Billing Act (15 USC § 1666) to the Truth in Lending Act (15 USC § 1601), and enforces more than 30 administrative rules. In the area of identity theft specifically, the FTC has additional statutory mandates. The agency is required, as noted above, to log and track complaints related to identity theft as a result of the 1998 Identity Theft and Assumption Deterrence Act. Additional responsibilities for the FTC arise as well under the Gramm-Leach-Bliley Act (15 USC §§ 6801–6809). That act mandates that the FTC, in conjunction with four other government agencies, ensure that banks and other financial institutions protect private consumer information.

To implement its various mandates in the area of identity theft, the FTC has created a three-pronged approach. The first is a toll-free telephone number that allows consumers to report identity theft. Counselors at the hotline can enter information provided by the victims as well as relay information concerning how to combat the problems associated with identity theft. The second and closely linked prong is the database and information clearinghouse already mentioned. The data entered from the hotline as well as data reported by other federal and state agencies are compiled here. Data collected and analyzed by the database and clearinghouse are used by the FTC to engage in the third prong of its approach: consumer and business education. This education has been undertaken through the publication of informational booklets such as *Identity Theft: When Bad Things Happen to Your Good Name* (2000), which can be found at the FTC maintained website at http://www.consumer.gov/idtheft. As a related but separate educational initiative, the FTC has also begun working closely and collabora-

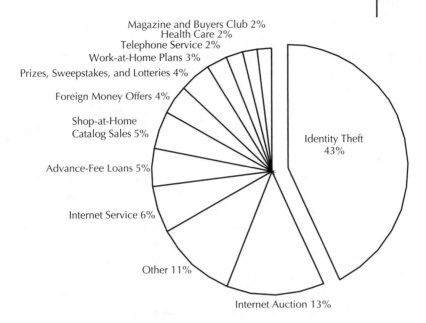

Magazine and Buyers Club 2%
Health Care 2%
Telephone Service 2%
Work-at-Home Plans 3%
Prizes, Sweepstakes, and Lotteries 4%

Foreign Money Offers 4%

Shop-at-Home
Catalog Sales 5%

Advance-Fee Loans 5%

Internet Service 6%

Other 11%

Identity Theft
43%

Internet Auction 13%

FIGURE 2. Top Fraud Complaint Categories—2002
Data represent total identity theft complaints to the Consumer Sentinel database January 1–
December 31, 2002, from information in the 2003 FTC report on fraud and identity theft.

tively with both law enforcement at the state level and private industry.

The role of the Social Security Administration in the federal effort is primarily one of information gathering. As mentioned already, the SSA operates a hotline that allows consumers to report fraud or theft related to their Social Security number or misuse of the system. Prior to February 2001, the SSA hotline did not have a category specific to identity theft, and hotline workers routinely categorized this crime as either "SSN Misuse" or "Program Fraud." An analysis of the 16,375 complaints lodged in those two categories from 1997 through 1999 determined that 81.5 percent related directly to identity theft.[13] Once an "Identity Theft" category was created, the response was immediate. From March through September of 1999, the SSA hotline logged 25,991 calls alleging identity theft, with the volume of calls per month increasing almost 40 percent during that period. In addition to the fraud hotline, the SSA also maintains additional information and resources for consumers on its website that is located at http://www.ssa.gov/pubs/idtheft.htm.

The Department of Justice (DOJ) involvement with identity theft is twofold. The first of the avenues of involvement is through the Executive Office for United States Attorneys (EOUSA), and the second major component is the investigative action undertaken by the FBI. Housed within the DOJ, these two agencies work closely together to investigate and prosecute identity theft as defined by The Identity Theft and Assumption Deterrence Act of 1998 and its amendments (18 USC § 1028 (a)[7]) as well as a host of related crimes under various other sections of the US Code (USC) including Social Security number misuse and fraudulent use of identification documents.

EOUSA data show that the office has been very busy in recent years prosecuting individuals for identity theft or closely related crimes and that the number of cases has been rising. In fact, the number of cases filed by EOUSA nearly doubled from 1996 to 2001 from 1,548 to 2,172 filings. It is difficult to determine whether these numbers are accurate representations of the total number of identity theft cases being pursued by EOUSA. Criminals have been and continue to be charged with crimes related to identity theft under a number of different statutes, and if the identity theft is part of a larger criminal enterprise, the defendant may be charged under statutes related to their other offenses. Even if the data are capturing all of the cases of identity theft, impressive as they are, they hardly scratch the surface of the totality of the problem and therefore point again to the difficulty of tracking down and apprehending this type of criminal.

The FBI is the second component of the DOJ that works prominently in the area of identity theft. Retrieving data about FBI work in this area is an extremely difficult proposition. As was noted previously, in many cases the FBI does not consider identity theft to be a stand-alone crime. Because of this fact, cases that involve identity theft are most often categorized and tracked by the FBI on the basis of the crimes committed using the false identification. Even individuals involved in large identity theft rings may be charged with a related offense such as credit card fraud or bank fraud rather than the underlying crime of identity theft. Bearing in mind that significant limitation, it is still possible to examine the effect of the FBI on identity theft. The number of arrests made under the six major sections of the USC related specifically to identity[14] can provide an approximation of identity theft arrests by the FBI. The number of arrests in these six categories went from 458 in 1996 to 922 in 2000. Again, this provides only an approximation of the role that is being played by the FBI but points again to the rising tide of identity crimes in the United States. The FBI has made changes in its tracking and data gathering so that, in the future, it will be possible to track cases by subsection of the USC, which will allow data explicit to identity theft specifically (§ 1028(a)[7]) to be gathered.

The Department of the Treasury also plays a role in tracking and punishing identity thieves in the United States. Specifically, the IRS, the Secret Service, and the Financial Crimes Enforcement Network (FinCEN) all provide data to the FTC regarding their involvement in identity theft crimes. By far, the FBI and the Secret Service are the most important actors in the identity theft arena.

The role of the IRS is directed primarily at the use of false identities to claim tax refunds. Most frequently these crimes involve falsification of documents such as earnings or withholding documentation. As is the case with the FBI, the IRS does not keep good statistics on the number and severity of these types of schemes. The data reported to the FTC, however, suggest that in 2000, there were approximately 3,085 schemes attempted that were classified by IRS internal audit as having a high frequency of identity theft or identity fraud as a component.[15] These schemes involved 35,185 individual tax returns and fraudulently claimed refunds in excess of $783 million. The detection and enforcement efforts of the IRS prevented $757 million in fraudulent payments in that year.

The Secret Service has authority to investigate and make arrests for a variety of financial crimes. As identity theft is frequently part of a larger picture of financial crime, the Secret Service has become heavily involved in that arena as well and serves as the lead criminal enforcement agency for the federal government in identity theft. As with the FBI, the Secret Service seldom views identity theft as a stand-alone crime, preferring to view it as one facet of ongoing criminal conduct. As a conscious choice, the Secret Service has shifted its emphasis in enforcement away from low-level or individual identity thieves and has begun to focus on the large-scale and international identity theft rings. As a result of that shift, the number of arrests and closed cases has actually *decreased* for the FBI, dropping 28 percent between 1998 and 2000 and 37 percent in the same period respectively. However, also as a result of that shift in emphasis, the value of each case closed, as measured in actual fraud-loss dollars prevented, has risen enormously. Between 1998 and 1999, the fraud losses prevented per closed case rose from $73,382 to $108,476, an increase of 48 percent. The following year the rate per closed case rose an astonishing 101 percent. Clearly, stopping the large-scale or international thieves of identity can have enormous impact on the real costs to consumers.

A final federal-level actor that deserves attention is the Postal Inspection Service. Much identity theft begins with theft of mail or at involves at least fraudulent use of the U.S. Postal Service. Reported Postal Inspection Service investigations involving identity theft were up 67 percent in 2000 as compared with 1999.[16] These investigations included direct theft of the mail as a means a thief utilizes to secure documents or identifying information, as well as the use of the mail to order and obtain fraudulent credit cards or bank account access through checks or other means. The Postal Inspection Service also investigated the use of private mailboxes rented at public facilities and the sometimes illegal uses to which they are put. Arrests by the Inspection Service jumped a dramatic 36 percent between 1999 and 2000 as a result of increased emphasis on identity theft as a crime.

In addition to direct enforcement efforts, the Postal Inspection Service has initiated many educational programs. The "kNOw Fraud" effort is the most well known of these initiatives designed to educate consumers and postal customers of the growing prevalence and costs of identity theft. The goal of the initiative is to mail a postcard to more than 120 million homes in America with postcards containing information on the trends in postal fraud and information on how to avoid becoming a victim of identity theft through the postal system.

The multiplicity of actors dealing with identity theft at the federal level might seem at first glance to be a positive development. In some cases it may be. In other cases the usual problems of overlapping or conflicting jurisdiction and mission overlap and duplication can come to the fore. The additional problem currently at the federal level is the lack of consistent understanding of identity theft. Because the different agency actors view identity theft differently and are responsible to different statutory mandates, it is often not even possible for these actors to engage in data sharing and cooperation.[17] Without that sharing and accumulation of consistent data, it is still not possible to provide truly accurate statistics on identity theft frequency. The 1998 Identity Theft Act is, as we will see, a significant step toward unifying the various definitions of the crime of identity theft, and agencies are making individual moves toward better and more consistent tracking of data. If these trends continue, it may soon be possible to provide much better data in this area. Regardless of the exact frequency of the crime, it is certainly a major area of criminal activity, and by almost every measure, it is increasing. As the frequency increases and the schemes to steal and utilize identity become more sophisticated, the costs of those schemes rises also.

Identity theft is an enormously costly area of crime. It

targets the financial security of individuals directly through attendant crimes such as credit card fraud and bank and wire fraud. It thus inflicts real costs not only on the consumers who are targeted by these thieves but also on the companies and businesses directly defrauded. A third level of cost is incurred by the governments of the states and by the federal government. Investigation, prosecution, incarceration and post-release monitoring are all expensive propositions. It certainly makes sense for government to take the proactive and preventative role that it has in the area of identity theft but even those measures incur costs. A final category of cost created by identity theft is nonmonetary. Loss of confidence in the system or an unwillingness to participate in the rising trend of e-commerce has societal effects that are not easily quantifiable in dollars and cents but certainly have a secondary impact on the whole system.

The Costs to Consumers

The most visible category of costs is the direct costs to consumers. The data on real costs to victimized consumers come from two main sources. The best data source for national level information is, once again, the FTC database on identity theft. This is by far the most comprehensive data set available. The second source of data is private organizations that are trying to highlight the problems of identity theft and have begun to collect data on a more limited scale than the FTC data clearinghouse. Of these private organizations, the most active are the California Public Interest Research Group (CALPIRG) and the Privacy Rights Clearinghouse.

In most cases of identity theft and the fraudulent use of a stolen identity, the victims are not responsible for the fraudulent charges or the bounced checks once they have convinced the credit companies and their banks that they are not the ones who made the charges or wrote the checks. If they can accomplish that, the credit and banking industries, as we shall see in a moment, simply write those expenses off.

While not responsible for the crimes, the victims of identity theft do bear the responsibility for clearing their names and restoring their credit records to their former conditions. Out-of-pocket expenses for this can mount quickly. Copying documents, sending certified letters, making long-distance phone calls all contribute to the real costs paid by consumers. Many victims are forced by the severity of their situation to hire legal assistance, and some have opted to simply pay the debt run up in their name rather than fight the system to have it removed from their bills. Once an individual has his or her credit destroyed by identity theft and has liens placed on property against wages and salaries, it can be difficult to convince the government to provide tax refund checks or even veteran's benefits until the matter is resolved.

The data on costs collected by the FTC are provided by the victims themselves at the time they initially call the hotline number. In many cases the victim has not yet incurred any out-of-pocket expenses because he or she has only just learned of being a victim. So, for 97 percent of the complaints to the database, there is simply no data available on real monetary costs, or the victim reports zero dollars spent out of pocket. That is not to say necessarily that the victim never incurs expenses, only that he or she does not have any at the point of initial contact with the FTC database. For the victims who report real expenses, approximately 8 percent report costs in excess of $10,000 to repair the damage done. Another 8 percent report costs between $5,000 and $10,000, and 30 percent report that they have spent between $1,000 and $5,000.[18] The CALPIRG survey[19] of identity theft victims in California reported similar results but they were on a smaller scale than the national average. That survey, conducted in 2000, found an average out-of-pocket cost to victims of only $100, but those victims reported an average theft of only $800, far below the national average for loss in identity theft cases.

Along with the monetary costs of being an identity theft victim come the nonmonetary repercussions. Both the FTC database and the CALPIRG survey report significant amounts of expenditure on the part of victims. Fourteen percent of the callers to the FTC hotline report some amount of nonmonetary impact on their lives. While that number is low, as with the monetary costs, many victims have not yet incurred the totality of these costs at the time they call the hotline number. More than half of those reporting nonmonetary costs reported that they had been denied credit or other financial services. Twenty-six percent cited significant time expenses to resolve the problems created by the theft. Twenty-two percent reported being harassed by credit companies or debt collectors. And, most disturbingly perhaps, almost one in ten was the subject of a criminal investigation, trial, or even conviction stemming from the theft of his or her identity.

Even after incurring the real dollar and nonmonetary costs and taking an average of 23 months to resolve the damage, according to the CALPIRG survey, many consumers feel that the issues surrounding the theft have still not been fully resolved. In some cases it is not possible to file a complaint in all of the states where the criminal activities occurred. Many victims continue to have an ongoing feeling of lack of closure, particularly when the crime involved elements in more than one jurisdictional domain. This feeling that the system has not taken care of the problem leads to an ongoing and deeply held sense of invaded privacy and vulnerability that may be the most difficult cost for consumers to pay, but it is one for which they are left largely on their own by the system.

The Costs to Business

The costs of identity theft to the banking, credit, and financial services industries are truly staggering. The losses take three main forms: direct fraud losses, loss avoidance costs, and indirect costs. Direct fraud losses are losses incurred by these industries when someone creates a false credit account and uses it to purchase goods or services. For banks, these losses also include fake or forged checks. Loss avoidance costs include staffing of fraud hotlines and consumer education as well as interdiction and investigation of possible fraud. Finally, indirect costs are borne by these industries as a result of loss of consumer confidence in the system that leads to people opting out of the credit system or even using it less frequently.

A 2000 survey of banks[20] by the American Bankers Association reported that the total fraud losses for commercial banks in the United States was $679 million in 1999. That represented a 33 percent increase over the 1998 survey data. When the loss avoidance costs of $1.5 billion are added in, the total real monetary cost of bank fraud in the United States was approximately $2.2 billion dollars for 1999. In the two-year period between the first and second surveys, the total direct fraud losses had more than doubled. While not all cases of bank fraud involve identity theft, some banks surveyed[21] reported that up to 56 percent of their fraud losses were connected to identity. Given that the survey and the American Bankers Association use a fairly restrictive definition of identity theft, the numbers may actually be somewhat depressed. The same survey reported that banks considered identity theft to be the third greatest threat against the deposit account system, behind only check forgery and debit card fraud, with the latter two being frequent components of identity theft crimes.

Aggregate fraud losses related to identity theft for the two largest consumer credit associations, MasterCard and Visa, rose from $79 million in 1996 to more than $144 million in 2000,[22] an increase of 43 percent in that period. Again, these numbers may be somewhat depressed by the definitions employed by the two associations. The category of identity theft employed by these associations is much narrower than the definition employed by either the Secret Service or the FTC. The associations categorize only direct account takeover and some portion of fraudulent applications as identity theft. Other types of fraud are not counted in this category because they may not involve the complete assumption of the identity of another. As identity theft or assumption can be an element in many different types of fraud, it seems that this definition is too narrow and certainly depresses the totals reported.[23]

While these two associations alone account for almost 75 percent of the credit card market, other general purpose cards such as American Express, Discover, and Diners Club have a significant share. Also excluded are bank-issued credit lines and retail credit losses. The data on fraud losses for these smaller cards are not readily available, but it is reasonable to assume that the identity theft losses for these cards would be consistent as a percentage of total fraud losses with those reported by the larger associations. Those percentages have remained fairly consistent in the last ten years at between 9 and 10 percent.

Fraud prevention and resolution also forces credit card companies and banks to incur costs for fraud departments and dispute resolution services. Again, the dollar values of these services are enormous. While not every dollar spent can be traced directly to identity theft as the underlying crime, many of them can be. Expenses for fraud department staffing varied enormously among banks in 2000, and the variance is related directly to the size of the institution.[24] While the smallest banks in the United States spend less than $10,000 annually on fraud, the largest banks, those with assets in excess of $50 billion, are spending far more. Of the largest banks, 27 percent reported spending in excess of $10 million annually on fraud-related matters.[25]

Other expenses that financial institutions and credit providers incur include increased customer relations expenses as a result of identity fraud and identity theft. While there is no dollar value available, banks and credit card companies are certainly devoting increasing amounts of resources to the assisting of customers who have been victims of identity theft. The companies are also devoting resources to cooperative efforts with investigating agencies when identity theft is recognized. Banks in particular spend significantly in attempts to collect restitution from thieves of all types, including thieves who use fraud and identity theft to perpetrate their crimes. Finally, these financial institutions pay an opportunity cost when they are victims and when they utilize resources to combat and rectify identity theft. Every dollar spent on these issues is a dollar that cannot be used to extend credit to a legitimate consumer, a lost opportunity for business and for profit. That is the cost that is most difficult to calculate.

The Costs to Government

As is the case with every other area of identity theft, the actual costs incurred by the various levels of government are difficult if not impossible to measure precisely. Agencies at the federal level have only recently begun to keep track of identity theft costs as a separate category. While the GAO has reported some cost data[26] for investigation, prosecution, and incarceration, those data should be viewed as "best guess" positions by that agency. That best guess is often predicated on cost data for white-collar crimes generally. Because of the complexity of identity theft and the frequently cross-jurisdictional or even transnational nature of the crimes, those estimates may undervalue significantly the costs of investigating identity theft specifically.

Governments at both the state and the federal level certainly do spend considerable amounts of money to fund the investigatory, prosecutorial, record-keeping, and educational functions that have been discussed already. In addition, the government suffers some direct losses through fraud, particularly tax and Social Security fraud. The federal corrections system, charged with incarcerating the offenders and supervising them after release, must also expend considerable resources in those efforts. As with individuals, some of the largest and most pernicious costs may be nonmonetary.

The FBI has reported that the average cost to investigate a typical white-collar crime is approximately $20,000. While identity theft falls generally into the category of white-collar crime, it may not fit into the average case cost very well at all. Identity theft is seldom an isolated crime. Rather, it is often part of a larger and more complex investigatory picture, for the FBI or any other agency. It is not unreasonable to suspect that the average cost for identity theft as a subset of white-collar crime would be higher, but the FBI does not have data to support or reject that specific assertion.

For other agencies involved in investigations, the cost data picture is even less clear. The Secret Service provides a "best estimate of average cost" of a financial crime but acknowledges that it does not track investigatory costs on a per-case basis. The average Secret Service cost estimate for all financial crimes was approximately $15,000, but that number must obviously be considered as dubious. Even fewer data are available from the SSA, which has an information system that does not allow tracking of time spent by function. The SSA argues that the average cost of identity theft is much greater for the general public and for financial institutions than for itself and that, in any case, the real cost to law enforcement is a moving target. Where that number is at any given moment reflects primarily a decision on the part of policymakers. It would be possible for the SSA or other investigatory agencies to devote nearly 100 percent of its budget to identity theft and other financial crime. That they do not decreases the costs but not the problems of that type of crime.

Prosecution and incarceration of those arrested for identity theft and related crimes are a second major category of costs for the government. The EOUSA is not able to isolate the cost of prosecuting identity theft cases but is able to provide an estimate for financial crimes generally. Based on what they admit to be an inexact methodology, they provided to the GAO a figure of $11,443 per prosecution, a number based on all 13,720 white-collar crimes handled during the 2000 fiscal year. While incarceration of criminals is generally an enormously expensive undertaking, white-collar criminals are marginally less expensive than violent criminals because they are housed primarily in minimum security prisons. The average cost per inmate in these prisons is $17,403 annually, and that figure is probably close to the annual cost of incarceration for a convicted identity thief. As a total cost to the system, incarceration depends greatly on the usual factors of plea bargaining, sentencing recommendations, and the vigor of the investigatory and prosecutorial components.

Conclusions

As the title of the GAO report suggests, the prevalence and cost of identity theft seem to be growing. There are, however, some important caveats to determining by how much. The prevalence data available are scanty at best. The only consistent source of data for identity theft is the data clearinghouse established by the FTC as part of its mandate under the 1998 Identity Theft statute. While the best source, even that database is far from ideal. It relies entirely on self-reporting on the part of victims and generates data only at the point of initial contact with the victim. As the database continues to grow and as other agencies begin increasingly to provide more meaningful cross-linked data sources, the benefit of the FTC information will increase rapidly. What is missing in the data picture at the moment is good reporting of data on state-level incidences of identity theft. That too is beginning to change as more states enact identity theft statutes and more state law enforcement agencies become part of the reporting system at the FTC.

Cost data are equally problematic in many ways. Most government agencies have only recently begun to view identity theft as a stand-alone crime that needs to be tracked. Those agencies are simply not yet equipped to provide real, meaningful, and reliable data of this specific component of the national crime picture. Private financial institutions have a nearly impossible task of unraveling identity theft from the other associate financial crimes committed by identity thieves. Credit providers are losing significant amounts of money annually and are spending enormous sums on loss prevention, but they are not yet in a position of feeling a sufficient negative impact on profits. Credit providers, while concerned about losses, will probably not begin to track identity theft very carefully until that theft begins to seriously impact their financial bottom lines.

Identity theft is increasing in cost and prevalence even as law enforcement and the criminal justice system strive for ways to stanch the flow. Advances in technology as well as changes in the statutory situation may provide some help. Those changes may also, at least in some cases, do as much harm as good.

CHAPTER 3

Information and Technology: Problem and Promise

Technology and Identity

That technology and identity theft are intimately related is an almost unavoidable certainty. The demise of personal recognition and the rise of the modern system of man-made, random numerical identification created a situation ripe for exploitation. The advent of the electronic database and the subsequent linking of databases have allowed identity thieves to operate more easily. The accident of these databases being tied together primarily through a single Social Security number has only added to the problem. The widespread and widely accepted use of electronic credit makes mistakes and even fraud much harder to catch and correct. And finally the creation, public acceptance, and ubiquitous nature of the Internet in twenty-first century America has multiplied the problems of all of these technologies many times. As a society, in our quest for online banking, online shopping, online bill paying, and online living, we have created a situation in which the very system on which we rely for easy use and convenience has become our own worst enemy. We flood the various systems with our most private information. Names, birth dates, employment, credit card numbers, and much more fly quickly through myriad channels intended certainly for a very restricted audience. That others may be watching the information flow seldom occurs to most of us until it is too late.

The rapid rise and linking of technologies has certainly created an enormous boon for the would-be or even well-established identity thief. He or she can gather more "private" information about an individual than was available even 50 years ago and can do it with amazing rapidity. The advent of cheap, powerful, and readily available personal computers capable of feats unheard-of only ten years ago and the ease of Internet access have made the process even more "criminal friendly." Put simply, nearly every technological advance that we have experienced in the past 50 years has worked to the advantage of identity thieves. Even worse, no one realized it. Many of us who use computers and even the Internet on a daily basis are woefully unprepared for the realities of these technologies, and government was caught similarly unawares. Until thieves had developed sophisticated methods of exploiting those technologies, until they had evolved a huge lead in the game, and until the problem became nearly monumental in scope, government did little to try and combat the problem. Once the problem became large enough, government decided to step in, but by then, in many ways, it was already too late for the relatively tame approach first tried.

As we will see in later chapters, governments at every level have been working hard to remove some of the technological advantage enjoyed by these criminals. The federal government continues to pass more and more sophisticated laws designed to criminalize these high-tech crimes as well as their precursors. States, while lagging even further behind, have begun to undertake innovative new strategies to stem the electronic flow of vital and private information into the hands of these criminals. Unfortunately, government has been fighting the battle against heavy odds. Having missed the genesis of the problem, the laws that have been passed have been attempts to play catch-up in a very fast moving game of high technical sophistication and even more rapid evolution. Even as government outlaws activities or closes loopholes in existing law, the criminal elements, far from complacent, are finding new means of utilizing the existing technology and also of pushing the legal envelope. The tools that have been given to law enforcement have not yet been sufficient for those agencies to make any serious inroads against this multibillion-dollar crime. That bleak picture may slowly be starting to change, however.

The same wave of technology that has allowed the rapid growth of cybercrimes, including identity theft, may finally be turned to the advantage of law enforcement agencies. A move on the part of government and private enterprise toward high-tech identification techniques and enhanced computer security has begun. Strong encryption software and biometric recognition programs have begun to come out of the science fiction novel and appear in the marketplace. The push to get these types of countermeasures in place was spurred in important ways by the events of September 11, 2001. The revelation that, although living primarily under their own identities, many of the hijackers had utilized stolen identities was shocking. That these terrorists, several of whom appeared on watch lists, had walked unnoticed and undetected through busy airports was unacceptable. These facts not only brought to light the role of identity thefts in international crimes including terrorism, but also sparked massive efforts to tighten the technology of the information net through which these people had slipped.

Biometrics is a return in a high-tech manner to recognition-based identification. It relies on machines to recognize physical characteristics that are unique to an individual—characteristics impossible to duplicate. Biometrics has been evolving for years but it has been given more attention since the terrorist attacks of September 11th. Government and private business are searching in earnest for new means of regulating access to physical locations such as secure areas of airports but also to sensitive electronic data. The challenge for these efforts is to strike a balance between necessary levels of security and desired levels of speed, cost, and ease of use.

Samples of some forms of biometric identification that are currently being developed or used are listed below.

Eyes—Both the iris and the retina can be used for identification. Every iris has a unique pattern—even between the right and left eye of a single individual. The patterns of the iris are very stable over time and are nearly impossible to fake or replicate. Iris recognition is already in use by some banks in the United States as an alternative to personal identification numbers (PIN). Patterns of blood vessels in the retina are also unique but they are less stable. In particular, they change rapidly after death. The necessity of having a bright light shone into the eye makes the identification more difficult and more uncomfortable. Retinal scans are best suited to very high security applications.

Face—The face of an individual can be mapped on the basis of specific points and their geometric relationship. For instance, the distance between the pupils of the eyes is a specific measurement and series of these measurements can create a picture of a mathematically unique face—a face that can be compared to others in a database. This type of system is already in place in many businesses from banks to casinos. It can be done from a distance and even without the knowledge of the person being scanned, but it can be fooled more easily than other systems and it can have significant error rates based on things such as the angle of observation.

Hands—Hands have long been a source of information for biometric identification, particularly the use of fingerprints. New technology now allows video images of a fingerprint to be captured and finger scanning is already being used by many banks and other businesses including hotels and supermarkets. An easy means of identification, finger scanning technology may also be very easy to fool. A more secure but more costly hand identification technology involves hand geometry—three dimensional hand images. This type of system was used at the 2002 Winter Olympics in Salt Lake City to verify the identity of athletes.

Others—Other biometric means of identification being developed include some more obscure techniques. Ear shape, voice dynamics, keystroke cadence when typing, deoxyribonucleic acid (DNA), and even body odor are nearly perfect biometric identifiers and may someday be used in practical day-to-day applications.

While probably an effort in the right direction, the use of technology to combat identity theft or any other crime is not without risk. As we shall see, reliance on and belief in technology is what got us to this point, and blind belief in the ability of technology to extricate us may not be the answer either.

Information and Identity

For identity thieves to function, they need personal identifying information about their intended victims. They need to have access to a steady source of individual identifying data in order to keep their scams operating. Fortunately for the identity thief, we live in an age when more and more of ourselves is being daily distributed in the public domain, and it is being distributed as man-made or random identifiers. We are less and less able to be truly private individuals in most cases and are nearly unable to exist as individuals outside of these man-made identifiers. We are forced by the realities of living in the modern world to accept that someone somewhere has control over large amounts of our identifying information. The necessity of our "identities" being so open is caused by several factors, but the most obviously important one of these is credit.

Most adults in the United States have credit. While not impossible to avoid, it is nearly so. Educational loans, car notes, and home mortgages are all credit with which most people come to have an intimate relationship that can extend for decades. To ensure that the people to whom they are extending credit are good credit risks, businesses quite reasonably want to know the past history of an individual's loans and payments, bankruptcies, and defaults. The compilation, organization, examination, and dissemination of this type of information were once handled by those businesses themselves. At most, the information might be handled by a local company that serviced several of the local business interests, and it consisted almost entirely of negative information. The local business or local credit reporting company only kept records only on people who had failed to pay their note or had defaulted in some other way. Whether handled by the business granting credit or by a local company, the information did not travel much farther in most cases than the edge of the town or city where the credit was granted.

The disadvantages of such a decentralized system were significant. A business in one town might grant credit to a bankrupt deadbeat from another town simply because the possibility or reality of data sharing did not exist. As credit became a more and more important and ubiquitous part of American life, the costs to businesses became substantial. In a capitalist society, if there is a service needed and money to be made from it, the service will arise. It was not long before large-scale national credit service and reporting bureaus were created to service not just local businesses but businesses across the country and even around the globe.

Credit bureaus do not actually grant any credit at all. They serve as clearinghouses for data that can be used to provide a legitimate service in the form of information to legitimate businesses trying to protect their assets. There are currently three primary credit reporting and servicing agencies in the United States,[1] with almost all local credit bureaus being subsidiaries of one of these three. The economies of scale that are realized by the largest national organizations make competition from or even the existence of small and truly local agencies nearly impossible.

These big three companies compile, maintain, and update credit information, good and bad, on nearly every adult in the United States. It is estimated by the government that as many as 170 million Americans, approximately 90 percent of adults, currently have information on file with at least one of the three credit reporting agencies, and most of those have information stored in all three. Far from just negative information, these agencies gather enormous amounts of information about individuals in an effort to make the reports that they are capable of generating more useful and valuable to the legitimate businesses they service.

A typical credit report contains more than just past payment history or bankruptcy information. A credit report contains the full name of an individual along with his or her birth date, Social Security number, current and previous addresses, employer information, all current and past credit accounts, and payment history on those accounts. Also included frequently is public records information, including court records such as bankruptcy filings, lawsuits, and negative civil judgments. Reading that list of information should be somewhat concerning. It reads like a laundry list of what a thief of identity needs to commit his or her crime. More disturbing still might be the fact that individuals cannot force these agencies to stop collecting this information.[2]

If the sum total of the uses to which individual private information is put were the servicing of legitimate clients, there would be little problem or cause for alarm. And, for many years, this was in fact the case. The Fair Credit Reporting Act made it illegal to provide to any nonsanctioned person or business any information contained in an individual credit report. Persons with purposes not statutorily approved were prohibited from receiving the information. Certainly violations of the act occurred, but in those cases investigations could find the perpetrators and punishment could be meted out.[3]

In the late 1980s, the Federal Trade Commission, acting in accord with the administration of President Bush, agreed to relax the privacy standard for information contained in credit reports. Account numbers and specific information about individual accounts including payment histories remained protected. Other information, known as "header" information, was given significantly reduced protection. After the FTC action, information contained in the header of a credit report could be freely sold by the credit agencies to nearly anyone who requested it.[4]

Usually costing less than $50, these header reports can provide an identity thief with more than enough information to get started on his or her crime.[5] If the thief does not know an individual's Social Security number, he or she can request an address lookup report. By supplying only the full name and address of an individual, the thief can obtain from an information broker previous addresses and Social Security number. This information then allows a thief to run what is known as a trace report. By supplying the Social Security number, the credit agencies or information broker can report the name, current and previous addresses, birth date, and employer and job title for every individual in their system using that Social Security number.

Of course the credit bureaus and the information brokers are not the only businesses compiling and disseminating potentially damaging information. Grocery stores and retail chains have started to create databases of consumer spending and other habits. Banking institutions are engaged in large-scale information gathering and sharing. The impetus comes from the desire to be able to direct-market to consumers in a more precise fashion, and the information collected by banks is often a good means of targeting specific individuals. Banks are required by federal law[6] to inform customers of their privacy policies and notify consumers of their right to opt out of having any of their private information shared with third-party marketers, but that provision has been notoriously weak. Failure to provide privacy and opt-out information should result in the bank losing its authority to share any information at all.

For a wide variety of reasons, most consumers never exercise their options to protect financial and other information from being sold by their bank to third parties. One of the most obvious reasons is that privacy policies and opt-out provisions are frequently complicated and difficult to understand for the average consumer. Banks have a financial disincentive to provide clear and easy-to-follow instructions for opting out. A 2002 report from CALPIRG[7] suggests that as few as 0.5 percent of consumers had opted out of information sharing. That same report notes that 22 percent of banking customers said that while they had received a notice of their privacy rights, they had not read it. At the same time, 41 percent reported that they could not recall receiving a notice at all.

Most of the time, the freewheeling exchange of information between financial institutions and third-party marketers has little real negative impact. Other than the annoyance of telemarketing calls or increased junk mail, there is little obvious negative impact. The real negative impact is in fact much more insidious and subtle. Once a bank sells your information to a third-party vendor, that information cannot be retrieved. It "belongs" to the purchasing company. That means that private individual information and its future course is governed by that company's privacy policies and agreements with the original seller. It may, if the policies and agreements allow, be sold and resold again and again. With each sale, the connection and control that the individual has regarding his or her private information becomes more diluted. Private information, information on spending habits, bank balances, and much more may make the rounds to any number of companies and individuals, some of whom may be fronts for identity thieves or other criminal operations.

The presence of credit reporting agencies and the propensity of banks and others to share information are an important parts of identity theft. The compilation in a single place of that much private information is a very dangerous thing. If information is the key to perpetrating or thwarting identity theft, then these institutions and practices certainly seem to favor the thief rather than the potential victim. While dangerous and potentially damaging, the information by itself would ordinarily be limited in distribution. That it is not is a function of a second problem, the relationship between all of this information and its flow through a system that is increasingly dependent on technology.

The Internet and Crime

Many people are fascinated by new technology even though most have, at best, a rudimentary understanding of how any of it works. Many of us are simply pleased to have instant access to Internet-based information on almost any subject we can imagine. We are excited by the possibility of online bill paying or online banking. We love the instantaneous nature and constant availability of the Internet and its related technologies. To facilitate those conveniences, we are willing on a nearly daily basis to provide private and sensitive information over the Internet without any real thought for the possible negative consequences of doing so.

That the technology of the Internet is becoming nearly ubiquitous is not hard to demonstrate. The number of Americans with Internet access continues to expand at a feverish pace. In the year 2000 alone, the number exploded, going from 75 million to more than 105 million individuals. And Americans continue to use the technology more and more. In 1995, there was only one bank in the United States that had a website capable of processing a routine transaction. Today nearly every bank offers online banking and bill paying. Between 1999 and 2000, the estimated value of online retail sales jumped more than 67 percent with those sales in 2000 having a value estimated at almost $26 billion.[8]

While many of us have become somewhat inured to the possible problems of the Internet and technology, the would-be thieves of identity have not. They have come to realize that these new technologies provide for them amazing new opportunities to engage in their criminal activities. These opportunities come both directly and indirectly.

Indirectly, the Internet benefits identity thieves because it is an enormous boon to information brokers. What was once a business that required traveling to government or corporate offices and looking through reams of files has been made considerably easier. An information broker no longer needs to visit any physical locations at all. More information is now available to these brokers and to their clients through a computer modem than would have been accessible even through physical searches of records.

As records of governments and businesses have become computerized they have also been cross-linked. The credit bureau header reports mentioned above can be cross-linked to many government databases. Voter registration information, property ownership, driving and vehicle ownership records, and professional licensing information are all legally available to the information broker through cross-linking databases. These brokers of information are not always law abiding in their approaches and methods, either. The FTC has targeted numerous brokers who were willing to use the information they could access legally to impersonate another person and thereby gain access to information to which they had no legal right.[9] And what is available to an information broker, from the comfort of his or her own office, is also available for a price to identity thieves.

The direct benefits of the boom in Internet traffic come from the willingness of individuals to provide sensitive and ideally private information over this new technology. Everyone agrees that the identity thief is very happy indeed to be able to take his or her scam "high-tech." The FTC reports that many scams, even those that have been around for years, are being reconfigured for use on the Internet and more that half of the fraud reports received by the FTC in 2002 had some connection to the Internet. This is all the more disturbing precisely because it preys on both the innate curiosity of newcomers to the Internet and the lack of knowledge that they possess. Everything from pyramid schemes to fake businesses designed to elicit credit card information are being tried now on the Internet, and with considerable success.[10]

The Internet also provides for the identity thief the ability to reach and to defraud many more people in a much shorter time. Digging through garbage cans looking for discarded credit card offers is much slower and more tedious than creating a website that offers credit or business opportunities to all who visit and provide some basic, though ideally private information. The Internet increases exponentially the speed with which thefts can occur, often faster than the criminal justice system can react to them. A website can be created, harvest hundreds or thousands of pieces of identifying information, and be dismantled before the victims, much less the police, are aware that a crime has been committed. The FTC has created a Rapid Response Team to combat the growth of Internet crime generally. The team has met with some limited success although it still takes at least a week for it to take action based on complaints received, too long in many cases.

The problem of speed is only compounded by the use of the technology itself to mask the crime and protect the criminals. Criminals can easily create false email addresses and fraudulent domain names to cover their tracks. Even if law enforcement does become aware of the activities, there may be no way to track the criminals once the website or email scam has folded up and moved on.

Of course for every garden variety theft that occurs on the Internet there is also a much more serious crime being committed. The FBI has been tracking violations involving the theft of identity on the Internet that involve bank fraud, credit card fraud, wire fraud, mail fraud, international money laundering, bankruptcy fraud, computer crimes and fugitive cases.[11] The Internet and computer technology have become a useful tool in the arsenal of nearly every type of criminal. Today's computers and software technology allow even a novice to produce realistic false identification documents with relative ease.[12] The availability on the Internet of templates for doing exactly that makes the job even easier. The ability to cheaply and easily become another person is invaluable to a thief. As a component of other crimes, then, identity theft is certainly on the rise.[13]

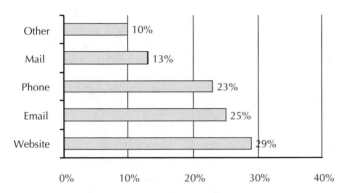

FIGURE 3. Thieves' Methods of Contacting Consumers
Data represent total fraud complaints to the Consumer Sentinel database where the method of initial contact was reported (77 percent of total complaints filed), from information in the 2003 FTC report on fraud and identity theft.

The International Link

It seems that globalization shapes everything in today's society, and identity theft is no exception. Some perpetrators of identity theft and related crimes rely on the Internet and technology to victimize people all over the world. The illicit trade of things such as stolen credit cards occurs daily on the Internet in readily accessible chat rooms:

> AntiOnline's 21-year-old founder, John Vranesevich, is monitoring a popular chat room where "carders" are trading filched account numbers. A message pops up from a carder using the online pseudonym—or handle—ELGOD : 'Wanna trade usa ccdz? I got 5 Visas, 1 mc, 1 Virgin Visas [sic].' 'Ccdz' are credit cards, 'mc' means MasterCard, and 'virgin' denotes a stolen number that has yet to be used illegally. . . .[14]

It appears that the Internet trading of illicit credit-card numbers occurs in a rather highly evolved black market, with traffickers participating all over the world. The perpetrators have even developed their own "language" to facilitate their illegal transactions, and their own marketing practices:

> Tens of thousands of stolen credit-card numbers are being offered for sale each week on the Internet in a handful of thriving,

membership-only cyberbazaars, operated largely by residents of the former Soviet Union, who have become central players in credit-card and identity theft. . . . The cost of a single credit card has been between 40 cents and $5 depending on the level of authenticating information provided. But the credit-card numbers are typically offered in bulk, costing, for example, $100 for 250 cards, to $1,000 for 5,000 cards.[15]

The illicit global trading of stolen credit card information presents a number of problems for law enforcement and for the judicial system. Some of these problems are theoretical, but some are very practical. As always, questions of jurisdiction arise. There is no law of cyberspace and no one person or government has jurisdiction over the Internet or crimes committed via the Internet. If phone lines are used in the United States in any portion of the crime committed, then technically the United States government and some state governments could claim jurisdiction to pursue prosecution of the crimes.

But it quickly gets more complicated if the American phone lines are never used. For example, if an American tourist loses his credit card in Yemen, and a criminal makes use of the card before the tourist realizes his loss, can American courts "reach" the criminal? It would depend on the circumstances. Practically, while there is a global marketplace, there is no consistent or uniform global law, and there is no consistent global law enforcement officer walking the beat. How are criminals outside the borders of the United States brought to justice? Practically, it is expensive and difficult. And that means that it usually does not happen. However, if the case is big enough, sometimes international thieves are pursued and caught.

American, British, and Canadian authorities cooperated to catch two alleged international thieves:

Two 18-year-old British men were in custody Friday after an FBI probe of millions of dollars in credit card theft through the hacking of e-commerce led investigators to Wales. The men allegedly used the screen name "Curador" to intrude into nine e-commerce Internet Web sites in the United States, United

Kingdom, Canada, Thailand and Japan. The FBI said the theft
involved credit card information from more than 26,000 accounts. The stolen credit card information was disclosed on the
Internet. Losses could exceed $3 million, authorities said.[16]

The United States, United Kingdom, Canada, Thailand,
and Japan each arguably had a claim to jurisdiction to bring
the alleged offenders to justice, as each country apparently
had victims of the fraud. Jurisdiction can get quite complicated, as treaties, which are yet another form of law, may
be implicated. Treaties covering jurisdiction and extradition
of criminals, including identity thieves, are beyond the
scope of this book, but it is important to point out the potential legal issue.

A second aspect of the internationalization of identity
theft that deserves to be considered is the role of identity
theft and fraud in activities of illegal aliens:

According to Immigration and Naturalization Service (INS) officials, the use of fraudulent documents by aliens is extensive. At
ports of entry, INS inspectors have intercepted tens of thousands of fraudulent documents in each of the last few years.
These documents were presented by aliens attempting to enter
the United States to seek employment or obtain other immigration benefits, such as naturalization or permanent residency
status. The types of false documents most frequently intercepted by INS inspectors include border crossing cards, alien
registration cards, nonimmigrant visas, and passports and citizenship documents (both U.S. and foreign). Also, INS has reported that large-scale counterfeiting has made fraudulent employment eligibility documents (e.g., Social Security cards)
widely available.[17]

The use of false or stolen documentation to enter the United
States is a considerable problem. Establishing identity for purposes of entering the country is a process that is considerably more complicated than establishing identity domestically. There are nearly 200 countries in the world that issue
unique passports, grant visas, and utilize official seals. In addition, more than 8,000 domestic government agencies
issue birth certificates, driver's licenses, or other documentation that can be used to establish citizenship or residency.

The large number of documents that must be recognized by border officials makes it easier for a fraudulent user to counterfeit one or more. Counterfeiting of identity documents on a large scale has begun to occur on the global market, and that is likely to increase in the future.[18]

While many aliens attempt to enter the United States in order to find a job or a better life, that is not the case with all of them. As we have all become more aware of since the terrorist attacks of September 11, 2001, some aliens are willing to use stolen or fraudulent identities to further much more serious international criminal activities. The "war" on terrorism will undoubtedly catch some international identity thieves. In fact, the United States has already been successful in stopping one international identity thief, Ahmed Ressam, and thwarting his plans for international terrorism, a case that will be discussed in a subsequent chapter. As with most cases of identity theft, however, the cases of international theft about which we know or that are successfully resolved probably represent only the tip of a rather large iceberg. Certainly the fact that many of the terrorists of September 11 had false identities they could use at will gives pause. And, while as a nation we have become very focused on international terrorism, terrorism is not the only international crime that is facilitated by stolen or fraudulent identities. Drug trafficking and smuggling are also tied closely to international identity theft.

As economics and identity theft become more and more global in scope, the latter becomes more and more difficult to combat both internally and externally. Cooperation is and will be a key to stopping the internationalization of identity theft. The cross- or multi-jurisdictional nature of many of the crimes makes it essential. The International Association of Chiefs of Police has called for increased international cooperation among policing agencies. In addition, the same technology that allows international thieves to operate may someday be used to catch them. In the near future, however, there are practical problems that make it difficult to bring international identity thieves to justice. It will take some luck, increased international cooperation, rapid advances in technology, and a lot of hard work.

The Technology Solution

Technology, and our increasing reliance on it, is certainly a contributing factor in many cases of identity theft. We utilize the Internet and use credit cards for many of our purchases. We allow our personal information to be collected and distributed widely in increasingly linked databases. Put simply, the technology of the twenty-first century has become a partner to the would-be thief of identity.

As the technology gap between the thief and those attempting to catch him or her has grown steadily larger, there have been calls to begin to utilize the technology that exists and even to develop new technologies that will aid in the fight against this and other "high-tech" crimes.

Many proposals for combating identity theft involve making private information more private, protecting it from those who would steal it. Certainly some of these efforts could help reduce the prevalence of identity theft. For example, making it illegal once again to sell even the header information from credit reports would make it much more difficult for thieves to obtain the information necessary to commit their crimes, although information on most of us is already so widely disseminated and available at this point that to retrieve it effectively is nearly impossible, the genie is out of the bottle. Nevertheless, criminalizing the sale of that information would have the benefit of protecting new consumers as they begin to amass a credit history with any of the credit bureaus.

A certainly valuable step would be the criminalization of the sale of Social Security numbers, a step that has been considered by the government already. Increasing the affirmative responsibility of businesses, particularly banks, in the area of privacy would help to solve the problem considerably. Strengthening consumer protection available under existing federal laws by, for instance, requiring an opt-in process for information sharing among businesses might help to stem the tide of information theft. Unfortunately, all of these steps would serve most likely to slow but not stop the growth of the problem. Even radical proposals such as generating entirely new and truly random Social Security numbers for every American can solve only part of the problem. The solution to identity theft is not going to be found in simply making information more and more difficult to obtain. If that tack is taken, the thieves will always be able to find a way to break into or buy their way into the database.

Any identifier that is not completely inalienable, even a newly created identifier such as a new Social Security number, can and will be compromised by the system. A new numerical identifier would be disseminated in the system as quickly as we used it to apply for a new credit card or to open a new bank account. Any new number created would have to be distributed widely to be useful. Once distributed, it would then suffer from the same problems inherent in the current Social Security number-based system. What is needed is the creation of a universally secure and efficient means of identification (USEMI). Most proposals for the development of this type of identifier are closely tied to the emergence of new technologies.

The emerging technologies rely on biometrics as a means of identification. Biometrics returns, in an admittedly high tech fashion, to the idea of identity based on recognition. Rather than relying on humans to do the recognizing, however, biometrics relies on machines. Some forms of biometrics are already being employed in several industries. Some banks and even supermarkets now have thumbprint recognition capabilities for accessing accounts or cashing a check. Airport security operations have begun testing facial recognition software[19] that can scan thousands of faces an hour. Matching the faces scanned by the computer to a database of known terrorists can aid enormously in catching criminals before they can act. Other systems being considered or tested include retinal scanners and even systems for matching DNA. The same technology currently being used in the 'war on terrorism' could also be employed in a war on identity thieves.

Imagine that rather than providing a Social Security number or a mother's maiden name to establish identity for a new credit card, it was necessary to provide a retinal scan or a DNA sample. Certainly identity thieves would have a much harder time stealing identities under those circumstances. That increased difficulty, however, might be offset by the increase in advantages to do so.

Biometrics may provide only the illusion of security while actually making the entire system more vulnerable. Remember that one of the problems with the current system is that nearly every personal identifier is linked at some point to the single Social Security number identifier. In the worst-case scenarios of identity theft, it may be necessary for an individual to obtain an entirely new Social Security number from the government to break the connection to the stolen identity.[20] While problematic and cumbersome, it can be accomplished. Imagine that, rather than a Social Security number, your identity was tied entirely to a thumbprint. If that thumbprint were compromised, it would not be possible to have a new thumb issued.[21] If that thumbprint were capable of accessing bank accounts, establishing lines of credit, securing entry or exit from a country, or even starting your car, the loss of that single feature would be more detrimental and harder to correct than the loss of a random nonbiometric feature of identification. Biometrics is, at this point at least, not able to provide a truly secure means of identification.

Clearly there are technological problems that need to be overcome before biometrics can be a useful tool in securing identity. There are also, however, cultural issues. We in the United States have a cultural aversion to surrendering any of our privacy. Many of us would view the necessity of submitting to a retinal scan or a DNA test to be overly invasive at worst or at best horribly inconvenient. Even the suggestion that the U.S. government issue identity cards to American citizens has been met with considerable resistance.

Conclusion

The modern world has created a system ripe for identity thieves. We have become more and more dependent on technology, and that technology has been increasingly exploited. The linking of databases, the sharing of information, and our willingness to participate in a flawed system have all contributed to the problem of identity theft.

Certainly the case of the individual identity theft victim is important. The costs to that individual and to the system as a whole are enormous and growing. The link to technology and the Internet have greatly expanded the scope of the problem and have led to the internationalization of identity theft. Used now by illegal aliens seeking employment as well as by international terrorists, identity theft has become far more than an inconvenience or even a scourge. It has become something that has the potential to subvert and destroy the entirety of the system of identity in the United States as well as all of the tangential systems that rely on identity to function.

Some of the solutions to identity theft may be found in technology. The perfect USEMI may be available and waiting to be developed. But, it is not here yet. Even if the perfect USEMI were found tomorrow, it would be necessary for people to accept and utilize the new identifier. Given the generally low rates of participation in the current systems designed to help consumers, it is unlikely that mass participation would be the result.

Until a solution is found, government and society are left in a position of having to utilize the existing system to its fullest advantage. The federal and state governments have begun to address the problem of identity theft in statutory enactments. While those enactments have met with some success, there is still much that can and should be done in that arena as well.

CHAPTER 4

Federal Laws on Identity Theft

The State of the Law

The statutory law regarding identity theft in the United States is enormously complex. Numerous statutes at both the federal and state levels may be applicable in cases of identity theft, identity fraud, and related crimes. The single most specific federal statute regarding identity theft is the 1998 Identity Theft and Assumption Deterrence Act. This act criminalized identity theft as a stand-alone crime and enacted stiff federal penalties. In addition to the federal level, 44 states have statutes dealing specifically with identity theft, and three others have similar laws pending. In addition to these identity theft-specific statutes, numerous other provisions in both federal and state law may also apply in cases of identity theft or identity fraud. That is almost certainly the case when that theft or fraud is part of a larger criminal enterprise or one component of an ongoing pattern of criminal activity. Taken all together, these various provisions facilitate numerous avenues for prosecution but they may also have the effect of muddying the waters considerably. In part because of the complexity of the law, identity theft can be a very difficult crime to prosecute.

Victims of identity theft may have remedies under both federal and state identity theft statutes. Therefore both levels of the system need to be addressed for a complete view of the statutory picture. The federal government has taken the lead in identity theft law, and as already discussed, many of the most important actors in creating and enforcing identity theft statutes are working in the federal government. Those federal actors are not alone, however, and state governments have increasingly recognized identity theft as a significant law enforcement problem and have begun to take steps to combat it. Because of the preeminent role that they play, it is necessary to begin with an examination of the federal identity theft statute and those related statutes that could most likely be relevant in these types of cases. It is useful then to examine state statutes regarding identity theft specifically as both a reaction to what has taken place at the federal level and as independent efforts in their own rights.

At the federal level, there are numerous statutes that deal with components of the identity theft problem, and many antedate the 1998 statute.[1] Even if they do not recognize it or attempt to address identity theft as a stand-alone criminal activity, the precursors to the recent enactments play an important role in setting the stage for the current statutory picture. This chapter will begin by looking at some of those early statutes in more detail. Federal efforts to combat identity theft or components of the crime include the 1974 Privacy Act, the Identity Theft and Assumption Deterrence Act of 1998, the Gramm-Leach-Bliley Act, the Truth in Lending

Act, the Federal Trade Commission Act, the bank fraud statute, the Social Security fraud statute, the credit card fraud statute, and the Electronic Fund Transfers Act.

Precursor Statutes to the Identity Theft Act of 1998

Congress took a first major step toward protecting privacy and preventing identity theft with a statute intended to protect the private information of individuals. By enacting the Privacy Act of 1974 Congress attempted specifically to protect "nonpublic personal information."[2] By the 1970s, agencies were beginning to routinely collect large amounts of sensitive personal information—base identifiers as well as the all important man-made identifiers—from their customers through regular business transactions. In order to protect this private and sensitive information, the Privacy Act of 1974 targeted primarily government agencies and allowed in part that government agencies could disclose information to the public, unless that disclosure of information could reasonably be expected to constitute an unwarranted invasion of personal privacy. Thus Congress imposed an affirmative duty upon government agencies to guard the private information of individuals.

Specific provisions of the Privacy Act of 1974 exclude from governmental disclosure personal sensitive private information in a number of instances, including trade secrets and commercial or financial information obtained from a person. Also specifically protected is information that is privileged or confidential, including personnel and medical files, the disclosure of which would constitute an unwarranted invasion of privacy, as well as information that could reasonably be expected to endanger the life or physical safety of any individual. Through the Privacy Act of 1974, Congress recognized the necessity of maintaining confidentiality of private information and took an important step toward protecting individuals' private information from unnecessary disclosure.

The Gramm-Leach-Bliley Act, passed in 1999, contains numerous provisions that significantly modify the notice requirements that must be met by financial institutions before they can share "private" customer information with other institutions.[3] The stated purpose of the Gramm-Leach-Bliley Act is "to enhance competition in the financial services industry by providing a prudential framework for the affiliation of banks, security firms, and other financial service providers, and for other purposes." This sweeping legislation, which allowed banks, securities firms, and other financial service providers to engage in each other's business, contains some provisions that are similar to those of the Privacy Act of 1974. Section 501 of Gramm-Leach-Bliley, for instance, addresses protection of nonpublic personal information. Congress reaffirmed in that section the general policy "that each financial institution has an affirmative and continuing obligation to respect the privacy of its customers and to protect the security and confidentiality of those customers' nonpublic personal information." Financial institutions also have a duty to protect confidential customer information.[4] Regarding a financial institution's disclosure of personal information to third parties, an institution, generally speaking, must provide notice of such disclosure, and in some circumstances give the consumer a chance to opt out of the disclosure.[5] Most consumers do not avail themselves of this option, however. The CALPIRG survey of bank privacy policies, for instance, reports that only 0.5 percent of consumers had actually exercised their opt-out rights.[6] The difference between this statute and the requirements of the Privacy Act of 1974 turns primarily on the numerous exceptions to the notice requirement of the Gramm-Leach-Bliley Act and the fact that Gramm-Leach-Bliley targets financial institutions rather than government agencies.[7] For a complete list of the exceptions to the notice requirement and applicability, one should consult the complete text of sections 502 and 503 respectively. Generally speaking however, the financial institution may be allowed, without giving notice to the consumer, to disclose nonpublic personal information if it is necessary to do so in order to carry out a transaction requested by the consumer, or to allow a third party to perform services for the institution—as long as the institution maintains a confidentiality agreement with that third party. The consumer can also consent to such information disclosure. Practically, the law allows financial institutions to use private information as necessary to conduct business, especially if the consumer requests the particular transaction.[8]

Section 521 of the act makes it a crime for a person to fraudulently obtain nonpublic personal information from a financial institution.[9] A violation of this criminal provision may result in up to five years in prison or a fine, or up to ten years in prison and a double fine if there are aggravated circumstances.[10]

Identity Theft and Assumption Deterrence Act of 1998

The reaction to a growing national problem of criminal identity theft combined with technological advances that facilitate criminals in committing identity theft has been specifically federal. The *Congressional Record* provides insight into congressional motive for adopting a specific federal law regarding identity theft. The House of Representatives considered the Identity Theft and Assumption Deterrence Act on October 7, 1998. Representatives Shadegg, DeLauro, Clement, and Sanders introduced the bill into the House. Regarding the act, Representative DeLauro, on the floor of the House, remarked in part that

> identity theft is growing. It is a harmful crime. It hurts the economy, it destroys consumer credit, and it places a burden on consumers to keep their identities under lock and key.
>
> It took a nightmare story from my own constituent, Denise, and Denise does not want her last name known because she continues to be frightened by what has happened to her and her family, to bring the issue of identity fraud to my attention.
>
> Denise contacted me 2 years ago and told me her story.

Thieves had used her stolen identification to access credit in her name in Rhode Island and again in Utah. The thieves made more than $2,000.00 in purchases and rented several apartments.

Denise has worked for more than 2 years to clear her good name and credit through multiple contacts with credit reporting agencies and an attorney. This identity fraud case has cost her a tremendous amount of time and huge sums of money.

The identity thief who stole her identity is continuing to use her identification to access credit in her name. In response to her case, and numerous other similar stories brought to my attention, I introduced the Identity Piracy Act to fight identity fraud.

Today, I am pleased to join forces with my colleagues to pass the Identity Theft and Assumption Deterrence Act. . .[11]

Clearly Representative DeLauro's constituent Denise and her case of identity theft influenced Representative De-Lauro to support federal law designed to combat the problem of identity theft. Other representatives spoke in favor of the proposed. Representative Hostettler was influenced by the plight of one of his own staff members, remarking in part:

I rise in strong support of this bill, a piece of legislation which, when discussed, may seem like something directly from the Sci-Fi Channel when someone would discuss theft of an identity and the assumption of that identity. . . .

In fact, earlier this spring, my district scheduler back in southwestern Indiana, Erica, experienced this very phenomenon. A person in Michigan had purchased information such as social security numbers and family information of Erica. The imposter then ordered a credit report to learn her credit status. After learning that status, and armed with that information, the perpetrator went on a 2-day spending spree, opened numerous charge accounts as Erica, and purchased in excess of $5,000.00 in goods, including the purchase of a cell phone.

The individual was caught only when a clerk noticed that the imposter hesitated at providing certain information and the credit card company called my district scheduler to verify it.[12]

The House of Representatives passed the bill regarding the Identity Theft and Assumption Deterrence Act on October 7, 1998. The Senate considered adoption of the identity theft law on October 14. In those deliberations, Senator Leahy remarked in part:

> This bill penalizes the theft of personal identification information that results in harm to the person whose identification is stolen and then used for false credit cards, fraudulent loans, or for other illegal purposes. It also sets up a 'clearinghouse' at the Federal Trade Commission to keep track of consumer complaints of identity theft and provide information to victims of this crime on how to deal with its aftermath.
>
> Protecting the privacy of our personal information is a challenge, especially in this information age. Every time we obtain or use a credit card, place a toll-free phone call, surf the Internet, get a driver's license or are featured in 'Who's Who,' . . . personal information . . . can be used without our consent or even our knowledge. Too frequently, criminals are getting hold of this information and using the personal information of innocent individuals to carry out other crimes. . . . The consequences for the victims of identity theft can be severe. They can have their credit ratings ruined and be unable to get credit cards, student loans, or mortgages. They can be hounded by creditors or collection agencies to repay debts they never incurred, but were obtained in their name, at their address, with their social security number or driver's license number. It can take months or even years, and agonizing effort, to clear their good names and correct their credit histories. I understand that, in some cases, victims of identity theft have even been arrested for crimes they never committed when the actual perpetrators provided law enforcement officials with assumed names. . . .[13]

The Senate passed the Identity Theft and Assumption Deterrence Act without amendment and by unanimous consent on October 14. The bill was then sent to the White House for the President's signature. The President signed the bill on October 30 and the bill became Public Law No. 105-318.

The Identity Theft and Assumption Deterrence Act of 1998[14] prohibits knowingly and unlawfully possessing and or using the identification information of another person. For the most egregious offenses involving possession of false identification such as facilitating international terrorism,

punishment ranges to a maximum of 25 years imprisonment. For less momentous criminal uses of identity, the
punishments can include a fine or imprisonment for up to a
year. Most violators of the federal identity theft statute could
receive 15 years in prison. This statute is important because
for the first time it makes identity theft a stand-alone federal crime. That in turn gives federal law enforcement a serious weapon with which to combat identity theft, which
occurs in a wide range of circumstances.

Internet False Identification Prevention Act of 2000 and the 2001 Sentencing Enhancements

The Identity Theft and Assumption Deterrence Act of 1998
was a good start in the area of federal legislation designed
to combat identity theft, but it had loopholes that criminals
were using. Under the original law, it was possible for criminals to produce templates used in the production of false
documents and traffic in the templates. These templates,
because they were not the documents themselves, were not
prohibited under the 1998 law, an obvious loophole in need
of closing. The Internet, combined with rapidly advancing
technology, allowed criminals to more easily than ever produce false documents using these readily available templates or other means. The Internet False Identification Prevention Act of 2000, passed by both the House and the
Senate, amended and strengthened the Identity Theft and
Assumption Deterrence Act of 1998.[15] The Internet act was
considered by the Senate on October 31, 2000. During the
deliberations on the bill, Senator Collins remarked in part:

> Mr. President, the high quality of the counterfeit documents
> that can be obtained through the Internet is astounding. With
> little difficulty, my staff was able to use Internet materials to
> manufacture convincing ID that would allow me to pass as a
> member of our Armed Forces, a reporter, a student at Boston
> University, or a licensed driver in Florida, Michigan, or Wyo-
> ming, to name just a few of the identities I could assume. For in-

stance, using the Internet my staff created a counterfeit Connecticut driver's license that is virtually identical to an authentic license issued by the Connecticut Department of Motor Vehicles. Just like the real Connecticut license, this fake with my picture includes a signature written over the picture and an adjacent "shadow picture" of the license holder. The State of Connecticut added both of these sophisticated security features to the license in order to reduce counterfeiting. Unfortunately, some of the websites offer to sell fake ID complete with State seals, holograms, and bar codes . . . virtually indistinguishable from the real thing. Thus, technology now allows website operators to copy authentic identification documents with an extraordinary level of sophistication and then mass produce those fraudulent documents for their customers. The websites investigated by the subcommittee offer a vast and varied product line, ranging from driver's licenses to military identification cards to federal agency credentials, including those of the Federal Bureau of Investigation (FBI) and the Central Intelligence Agency (CIA). Other sites offer to produce Social Security cards, birth certificates, diplomas, and press credentials.[16]

The Identity Theft and Assumption Deterrence Act of 1998 also delegates the primary responsibility for combating identity theft to the FTC.[17] The act of 1998 specifically requires the FTC to "(1) log the receipt of complaints by victims of identity theft; (2) provide identity theft victims with informational materials; and (3) refer complaints to appropriate entities, including the major national consumer reporting agencies and law enforcement agencies."[18] In response to these mandates, the FTC established a toll-free telephone number (1-877-ID Theft) that consumers could call to report identity theft. Counselors at that hotline advise victims of identity theft of their rights under the Truth in Lending Act and the Fair Credit Billing Act, which may limit their liability for unauthorized charges. The FTC also established a website at which consumers can report cases of identity theft and get comprehensive information regarding it.

Most significantly, the FTC established the Identity Theft Data Clearinghouse which can be accessed at the FTC website in order to log complaints and to build a database for cases of identity theft for use by law enforcement agencies, policymakers, victims of identity theft, and the public. As has been discussed, this data source has become extremely valuable to law enforcement and contains the most comprehensive data available on the prevalence and cost of identity theft as a crime. In order to help consumers inform the three major credit reporting agencies and other creditors, the FTC has also developed a single form, the ID Theft Affidavit, which can be filled out by the victim and used to inform the credit agencies and creditors of the identity theft, thus greatly reducing the amount of paperwork.

In response to the tremendous advancements in technology and tactics used by Internet providers of high quality fraudulent identification documents, Congress strengthened the Identity Theft Act of 1998 by adding or modifying a few key provisions of that law. The 2000 act provides for a more vigorous enforcement of the federal identity theft law by requiring that a coordination committee be established to ensure the "vigorous investigation and prosecution of the creation and distribution of false identification documents." Congress also required the attorney general and the secretary of the treasury to appoint a special committee, to exist for at least two years, comprising representatives from the Secret Service, the FBI, the DOJ, the SSA, and the Immigration and Naturalization Service (INS). The committee was charged with curbing the growth of false identity crime, and to report the results of agency actions on a yearly basis.

Importantly, 18 USC § 1028 was modernized by modifying the then-existing definition of "document-making implement" to include computer templates and files that were and are used frequently to create counterfeit identification documents from the Internet. A new provision made it illegal to "knowingly produce or transfer a document making implement that is designed for use in the production of a false identification document." This modification was intended to close a loophole in the prior law that allowed a person to transfer, through a website or by email, false identification templates that could easily be made into finished documents. A definition of a "false identification document" was also provided, defined as a document intended or commonly accepted for the purpose of identification that is not issued by or under the authority of a government but that appears to be issued. One of the remaining provisions repealed 18 USC § 1738, ending the loophole which allowed a producer of a false document to escape liability for production of the document by adding a disclaimer which stated "NOT A GOVERNMENT DOCUMENT." All of these revisions substantially strengthened the Identity Theft and Deterrence Act of 1998, by closing loopholes.

A separate section of the Identity Theft and Assumption Deterrence Act of 1998 required the United States Sentencing Commission to provide sentencing guidelines for the federal identity theft statute. After completing public notice and hearing requirements, the United States Sentencing Commission issued sentencing guidelines which "increased penalties for criminals who steal another person's identity and then use that stolen identity to commit additional crimes, such as obtaining fraudulent loans or credit cards. In so doing, the Commission recognized that the individual whose identity is stolen is also a victim of the fraud, just as is the bank or credit card company."[19]

The protection provided by the Identity Theft and Assumption Deterrence Act of 1998 is much broader than the protection provided by the Privacy Act of 1974, and it specifically makes identity theft a crime. The Identity Theft and Assumption Deterrence Act of 1998 also prohibits anyone, including private individuals, from illegally producing, transferring or possessing false identification with the intent to commit a crime. The criminal penalties for violating the 1998 act are also more severe than those in the 1974 act. For the most egregious offenses involving possession of identification such as facilitating international terrorism, punishment ranges to maximum of imprisonment for 25 years. For less momentous criminal uses of identity, the punishments can include a fine or imprisonment for up to a year. This is compared to a misdemeanor charge for an aggravated violation of the Privacy Act of 1979.

Other Federal Statutes Relevant to Identity Theft

While the 1998 Identity Theft and Assumption Deterrence Act is the single most important piece of federal law currently in place, it is not the only federal tool available to combat identity theft. In fact, the 1998 act serves in important ways to draw together other statutory provisions that together provide protection or relief from identity theft and its consequences. The U.S. Sentencing Commission reports that violation of as many as 180 different federal statutes may fall within the 1998 act.[20] Some of these other federal statutes can be used by prosecutors in particular fact patterns, and some federal statutes can be used by victims of identity theft in their efforts to repair damage done by identity thieves. The Truth in Lending Act is one federal statute aimed at protecting the rights of consumers.[21] The legislature noted that its purpose was to "assure a meaningful disclosure of credit terms so that the consumer will be able to compare more readily the various credit terms available to him and avoid the uninformed use of credit, and to protect the consumer against inaccurate and unfair credit billing and credit card practices." A victim of identity theft may need to resort to provisions of this law in order to deal with unfair credit card billings resulting from criminal activity related to identity theft or fraud. The Fair Credit Billing Act also contains a provision giving consumers the right to correct credit billing errors.[22] After the consumer notifies the creditor of the erroneous billing, the creditor must fix the error or send a letter of explanation stating why it believes the debt to be valid. If a creditor pursues collection of a debt in bad faith, the consumer can pursue civil remedies.[23] That does not mean, however, that the consumer's credit report will necessarily be cleared quickly or at all. Credit reporting agencies are specifically protected from liability for erroneous credit reports, provided that they follow a standard of reasonableness in producing those reports. The consumer also has the right to rescind some transactions under certain circumstances. Generally, a consumer has a "cooling off period" of at least three days in which to rescind a purchase made on credit in which the creditor retains a security interest.[24] If a victim of identity theft discovers that a criminal made a large secured transaction within three days of the transaction, the victim should be able to undo the transaction, thereby preventing the illegally made purchase from ever showing up on his or her bill or credit report. Unfortunately, it is the rare exception that an individual becomes aware of identity theft so quickly.

The Federal Trade Commission Act[25] gives the FTC broad power to combat unfair methods of competition. The act declares "unfair methods of competition in or affecting commerce, and unfair or deceptive acts or practices in or affecting commerce, are hereby unlawful."[26] The act then directs the FTC to prevent virtually anyone from using those unfair methods of competition, empowering that agency to seek civil liability for violations. Infringements could result in violators being fined up to $10,000 per violation. Anyone, including a criminal, who commits identity theft and in doing so commits a deceptive act affecting commerce faces liability under the Federal Trade Commission Act.

While identity theft should be viewed, in some instances at least, as a stand-alone crime, criminals do frequently commit identity theft in order or facilitate other crimes such as fraud or other thefts. Other specific types of fraud, namely fraud in connection with access devices, bank fraud, Social Security fraud, credit card fraud, and major fraud against the United States, are all prohibited by federal statutes and are all common activities associated with identity theft. If a criminal commits identity theft and uses some type of counterfeit access device in the process, the criminal faces liability not only under the federal identity theft statute, but also under other federal statutes[27] prohibiting the use of counterfeit access devices. "Whoever (1) knowingly and with the intent to defraud produces, uses, or traffics in one or more counterfeit access devices" shall be punished by a prison term of as much as 15 to 20 years and a fine.[28] Thus a criminal using a counterfeit access device and identity theft to perpetrate a fraud could face more than 30 years in prison under a combination of federal statutes.

Criminals who commit identity theft often do so in order to defraud a bank. Bank fraud itself is a serious federal offense, and the federal statute prohibiting bank fraud can be used also in cases of identity theft. The bank fraud statute, 18 USC Part I, Chapter 63 § 1344, states that:

> Whoever knowingly executes, or attempts to execute, a scheme or artifice,
>   (1) to defraud a financial institution; or
>   (2) to obtain any of the moneys, funds, credits, assets, securities, or other property owned by, or under the custody or control of, a financial institution, by means of false or fraudulent pretenses, representations, or promises; shall be fined not more than $1,000,000.00 or imprisoned not more than 30 years, or both.

An identity theft committed to further a bank fraud could land the criminal in prison for a maximum of more than 40 years, though judges are bound by sentencing guidelines that could result in a lesser sentence.

Identity theft is also commonly used in furtherance of schemes to defraud Social Security. Social Security fraud is a specific type of fraud involving a false statement in order to cause a Social Security payment to be made or increased. Those arrested and convicted could face a felony conviction, five years in prison, and substantial fines.[29] Again, if the perpetrator of an identity theft also commits Social Security fraud, the perpetrator may face prison time for both offenses. This is a good point at which to mention the Social Security Number Misuse Prevention Act of 2001. As of July 11, 2002, this legislation was still under consideration in the Senate.[30] The act, if it becomes law, will prohibit the display, sale, or purchase of Social Security numbers except in specifically allowed exceptions. This act, if passed, would create a private cause of action for violations and authorize civil penalties for a person who the attorney general determines has violated the act. The act would allow civil penalties, including monetary, for the misuse of a Social Security number and the act also contains criminal provisions. The act would drastically change the way that the government and society uses Social Security numbers. The Social Security Act would be amended to prohibit the use of Social Security numbers on checks, the appearance of Social Security numbers on driver's licenses and motor vehicle registrations, and access to Social Security numbers by inmates of penal institutions.

The most common type of identity theft is committed to carry out credit card fraud. Credit card fraud is in itself a serious crime prohibited by federal statute. The federal credit card fraud statute, 15 USC Chapter 41 Subchapter I, Part B, § 1644, contains stiff penalties:

> Use, attempt or conspiracy to use card in transaction affecting interstate or foreign commerce, uses or attempts to use any counterfeit, fictions, altered, forged, lost, stolen, or fraudulently obtained credit card to obtain money, goods, services, or anything else of value which within any one-year period has a value aggregating $1,000.00 or more . . . shall be [subject to a fine of] not more than $10,000.00 or [imprisonment for] not more than ten years or both.

Also, if a criminal commits a major fraud against the United States, for example by filing fraudulent federal income tax forms in order to induce federal income tax refunds, the criminal faces serious penalties. Major fraud against the United States is specifically prohibited by federal statute,[31] which provides for a fine, up to $10,000,000 and imprisonment for up to ten years.

The Electronic Fund Transfers Act also contains some provisions that may offer protection to victims of identity theft.[32] Unauthorized electronic transfers, stolen credit cards, etcetera, should be reported as soon as possible after discovery. With notification of theft, consumer liability for unauthorized electronic transfers is generally limited to between $50 and $500, depending on when the credit card issuer is notified of the unauthorized use.[33] A related section of the same law prohibits a waiver of rights; the consumer cannot waive rights created by the Electronic Fund Transfers subchapter, which provides more protections for the consumer. A powerful creditor cannot force a consumer to waive these rights. Two other provisions of this act establish criminal and civil liability for.[34] Civil liability could result in a plaintiff being awarded actual damages or up to $1,000. In a successful class action lawsuit under this statute, plaintiffs could be awarded up to $500,000 or 1 percent of the defendant's net worth, plus costs and attorney's fees. Criminal liability in cases involving a transaction affecting interstate commerce could result in a fine of up to $10,000 and or imprisonment for up to ten years.[35]

We should briefly discuss conspiracy. Conspiracy, generally speaking, is simply an agreement by two or more people to commit a crime, any crime.[36] The concept that conspiracy and the underlying crime are separately chargeable offenses is known as the Pinkerton rule, after the Supreme Court decision in *Pinkerton v. United States* in 1946.[37] Federal and state laws prohibit conspiracy, as defined above.[38] Perpetrators of identity theft often work in concert, and could be charged with conspiracy in addition to other crimes. Conspiracy provisions are thus a powerful prosecutorial tool.

Conclusions

As we have seen, there are numerous federal statutes that may be relevant in cases of identity theft. Since 1998, identity theft by itself has become a serious and specifically prohibited crime under federal law. And many specific types of fraud, like bank fraud and credit card fraud, are separate crimes under federal law. The federal statutory scheme allows a prosecutor to "throw the book" at an individual who commits identity theft in addition to many other serious crimes. Being able to throw the book at an accused often gives the prosecutor great leverage to negotiate a plea bargain. An individual charged with identity theft, credit card fraud, and bank fraud might be offered a deal. The prosecutor may offer to drop the identity theft charge if the defendant agrees to plead guilty to the credit card fraud and bank fraud charges. If the defendant agrees, the prosecutor saves the government the time, expense, and risk of a trial. The government is guaranteed a certain result, and the defendant faces certain prison time. If the case for the prosecution is strong, the defendant may reduce the time spent in prison as a result of the identity theft charge being dropped, and does not have to endure a trial. The end result of such a scenario benefits the government and society by ensuring that criminals are taken off the streets. Identity theft being recognized as a stand-alone crime—whether ultimately charged, bargained, or dropped—increases the effectiveness of law enforcement in investigating and making arrests in cases where identity theft is involved even if it is one part of a larger criminal enterprise. It helps also in the legal system, providing prosecutors with one more option in dealing with an ongoing epidemic.

While to this point the federal government has taken the lead in identity theft legislation, the future of legal developments may be from the bottom up. Senator Maria Cantwell (D-WA) is leading Congress in combating identity theft. Senator Cantwell previously authored the Identity Theft Victims Assistance Act that was not signed into law but did receive substantial Congressional support and she plans to introduce it again in 2003 with co-sponsor Senator Mike Enzi (R-WY).[39] According to Senator Cantwell "too often, victims of identity theft must become their own private investigators to clear their good name and the FTC's report shows the problem is only getting worse. . . . My bill will make sure victims get the records they need to protect their identities and financial security."[40] The act is modeled substantially on Washington State's innovative identity theft statute that is discussed in detail in the chapter that follows.

The proposed law would amend federal statute to allow victims of identity theft access to information from businesses so that victims could repair damage done by identity thieves.[41] The act would further amend federal law to allow state attorneys general to bring actions on behalf of residents of the state in federal district court. The act would also allow the attorney general of the United States to intervene in those cases. Finally, the act would amend the Fair Credit Reporting Act to allow for a consumer to request that a block placed on the victim's credit report to exclude faulty credit information resulting from identity theft.[42] The act also "extends for victims of identity theft, the statute of limitations for the Fair Credit Reporting Act [to] four years, rather than the current two, addressing the Supreme Court's decision in *TRW v. Andrews*,"[43] a case discussed in chapter six. As proposed, The Identity Theft Victims Assistance Act would be a logical extension of federal law to further help victims and law enforcement combat identity theft.

CHAPTER 5

State Laws on Identity Theft

State Statutory Provisions

State laws have followed in the wake of the federal government's efforts. Forty-four states have statutes in place that address some components of identity theft and related crimes. However, prior to the enactment of the 1998 federal statute, only a handful of states had identity theft-specific statutes on the books. In 1999, in the immediate wake of the federal law, 22 states adopted relevant identity theft–related statutes and today 44 states have such statues on the books. By June 2002, FTC analysis of state laws[1] indicated that identity theft could be charged as a crime in 45 of the 49 states that had relevant laws on the books.[2]

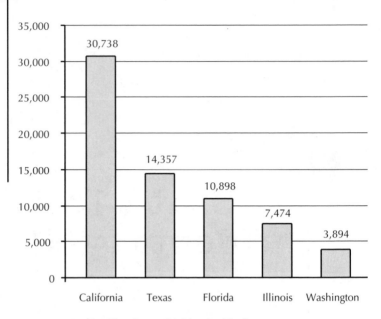

FIGURE 4. Top Five States for Identity Theft
Data from Consumer Sentinel Database information in the 2003 FTC report on fraud and identity theft.

In addition to the numerous federal statutes related to identity theft, state laws regarding identity theft have also proliferated in the last ten years. Most states now have specific statutes prohibiting identity theft and various types of fraud, similar to and augmenting the federal statutory scheme. Thus, state prosecutors can in many cases also "throw the book" of state laws at the accused. There is certainly no single, universal, or uniform state law regarding identity theft. It is difficult therefore to talk about "state laws" as they relate to identity theft. However, examination of some of the most innovative state statutes can provide some insight into how states are addressing the problem of identity theft. It is most useful to examine statutes in California, Florida, Illinois, and Washington as these all provide good examples of the scope of the identity theft problem and how that problem is being dealt with by state legislatures. In fact, California, Florida, and Washington represent three of the ten states most impacted by identity theft.[3]

While sharing a relatively common impact from identity theft, all four states vary considerably in their approaches to setting statutory punishment for violation of their respective identity theft laws. Some states punish criminals who violate identity theft laws as felons, by sentencing them to more than one year in prison. Some states, like California, punish violations of identity theft laws as misdemeanors, or as gross misdemeanors, by sentencing criminals for up to one year in prison. States often impose fines on the criminals as well, potentially thousands of dollars.

California Statutory Law Regarding Identity Theft

California passed a law addressing identity theft in 1997. In that law, California penalizes violations of the identity theft statute as a misdemeanor, with imprisonment not to exceed one year, and or a fine of up to $10,000.[4] The only felony provision in the California identity theft statute applies to individuals who falsely impersonate another in marriage.[5] Although the criminal penalties for violating California's identity theft statute are relatively weak, the law contains unique provisions that are noteworthy.

Victims of identity theft spend hours trying to restore their lives and undo the damage caused. Victims needed a law to assist them in their battle to restore their lives. It is frequently the case that victims of identity theft are treated almost as badly as the perpetrators of the crime. They are usually abandoned by a system that has not yet come to terms with the crime committed against them. In many cases these victims are left to spend years of their own time and thousands of dollars of their own money to have their records and names cleared. The California identity theft law contains a specific provision that directs that court records be corrected to protect the innocent victim.[6]

Giving courts this specific power to issue an order stating that the victim is not responsible for committing the crime helps crime victims restore their lives; they can offer a court order proving their innocence to current or future creditors, employers, and others. While that order may not erase all of the pain and problems, it can certainly go a long way toward creating the feeling of "closure" that so many victims of identity theft say that they have not achieved.

These days there is tremendous pressure on law enforcement to investigate and prosecute crimes, while law enforcement has limited resources.[7] Accordingly, it must set priorities. Since September 11, 2001, law enforcement at all levels, but especially the federal level, has placed countering terrorism as its number one priority. Fighting the war on drugs has been another significant priority of law enforcement for many years. Crimes that endanger the physical safety of individuals, like murder, rape, and robbery, also receive high priority. In the face of these obvious physical threats to individuals or to society as a whole, it is perhaps not surprising that a crime often perceived as white-collar or high-tech or one that is frequently thought of as minor or even victimless, like identity theft, would receive less attention from law enforcement agencies.[8]

The aftereffects of the terrorist attacks on September 11 not only changed the nation's law enforcement priorities, but have also been tremendously deleterious for the economy. The country may have had, and may have significant economic troubles. Some troubles are independent of those caused by the terrorist attacks, but, many are linked to it. So, a combination of limited and shrinking law enforcement resources and a shift in priorities elsewhere leaves state and local law enforcement heavily burdened and spread thin. Consequently, an "identity theft" crime, without there being more to it, without being attached to a terrorist incident or homicide, may not receive much attention from law enforcement. Victims of identity theft sometimes have trouble getting police to even take a report about the crime, let alone having it investigated and prosecuted. The California statute, enacted prior to September 11, gives identity theft victims in California some leverage with their local police departments. The law contains a specific provision requiring that police take a report of identity theft and that they investigate all allegations of it.[9] All states would do well to model a law upon this provision.

Normally in the American legal system there is no way for a victim to obtain a factual finding of innocence. In the civil court system such a victim is usually found liable or not liable, but not innocent. Similarly, in the criminal justice system, an accused is usually found guilty or not guilty. None are found innocent. However, California's identity theft statute allows the victim to petition the court for a factual finding of innocence.[10] That a victim may do so is a new development in American law. A factual finding of innocence further vindicates the victim, serves the interest of justice, and may provide some additional leverage for the victim in attempts to restore his or her credit standing. The victim can use the factual finding of innocence to help rebuild his or her life. Obviously, it is possible for identity thieves to fraudulently misuse even this provision of the law for their nefarious purposes. If that occurs, the court can revoke the factual finding of innocence, and the perpetrator if caught is in a lot of trouble and could face liability under the identity theft statute as well as fraud charges and possibly be held in contempt of court. California's statute regarding identity theft contains creative provisions that attempt to deal proactively with the problem of identity theft, to force police departments to look at it as a serious crime, and offers real help to victims in rectifying the real harms done them. While different in many of its specifics, Florida's statute also offers a new approach that states should be taking seriously as they begin to create new and better identity theft statutes.

Florida Statutory Law Regarding Identity Theft

Florida passed a law pertaining to identity theft in 1999.[11] Florida's identity theft statute penalizes violations as misdemeanors for lesser offenses, and as felonies of various levels depending on the amount of harm caused by the criminal. The more economic harm the criminal causes, the more serious the felony charges he or she faces.

> Any person who willfully and without authorization fraudulently uses, or possesses with intent to fraudulently use, personal identification information concerning an individual without first obtaining that individual's consent, commits the offense of fraudulent use of personal identification, which is a felony of the third degree. . . . Any person who willfully and without authorization fraudulently uses personal identification information concerning an individual without first obtaining that individual's consent commits a felony of the second degree . . . if the pecuniary benefit, the value of the services received, the payment sought to be avoided, or the amount of the injury or fraud perpetrated is $75,000.00 or more.[12]

Florida's statute attempts to achieve proportionality between the crime committed and the punishment for that crime.[13] A criminal convicted of identity theft solely for the purpose of harassment, for instance, faces a misdemeanor and no more than a year in prison. On the other hand, a criminal convicted of a major felony under Florida's identity theft statute faces imprisonment for up to five years and or a fine of up to $5,000 and could be required to pay up to double the pecuniary gain of the defendant or loss of the victim. All states attempt to achieve proportionality of some kind in their criminal statutes, but Florida's identity theft statute achieves a particularly good balance because it draws a reasonable distinction among misdemeanor identity theft, felony identity theft, and major felony identity theft. Justice requires proportionality between the crime committed and the punishment imposed. Arguably, the Eighth Amendment, which prohibits cruel and unusual punishment, also requires that crimes and punishment be proportional, and the Florida statute achieves a Constitutional balance between crime and punishment.

The statute contains another provision, regarding restitution. Although not unique to Florida, its identity theft law has a provision that allows the court to order that the criminal pay restitution to the victim.[14] The restitution payment could include reimbursement to the victim for attorney's fees, court costs, and other out-of-pocket expenses as the court determines to be just. Florida's identity theft statute is well written, and Illinois' identity theft statute contains some noteworthy provisions as well.

Illinois Statutory Law Regarding Identity Theft

Illinois passed a statute addressing identity theft in 1999.[15] The Illinois statute penalizes criminals who commit identity theft with maximum sentences ranging from 1 to 30 years in prison. Like Florida, Illinois also attempted to employ the principle of proportionality in the identity theft statute ultimately adopted. There is a twist to the Illinois approach, however. It treats most classifications of identity theft as being punishable as felonies rather than allowing many to be charged as misdemeanors. The more valuable the property taken by the identity thief, the more serious is the felony and the greater the maximum sentence possible. That is typical. However, Illinois incorporates the criminal's previous record as a way to enhance repeat offender sentences. A first-time offender may get a break under the Illinois scheme, but repeat offenders are dealt with severely:

> Financial identity theft of credit, money, goods, services, or other property not exceeding $300.00 in value is a class A misdemeanor. A person who has been previously convicted of financial identity theft of less than $300.00 is guilty of a Class 4 felony. . . . Financial identity theft of credit, money, goods, services, or other property exceeding $300 and not exceeding $2,000 in value is a Class 4 felony. . . . Financial identity theft of

credit, money, goods, services, or other property exceeding $2,000 and not exceeding $10,000 in value is a Class 3 felony. . . . Financial identity theft of credit, money, goods, services, or other property exceeding $10,000 and not exceeding $100,000 in value is a Class 2 felony. . . . Financial identity theft of credit, money, goods, services, or other property exceeding $100,000 in value is a class 1 felony.[16]

Often a state will issue a statement regarding the public policy reasoning behind the adoption of a particular law. The state of Illinois undertook such an explanation in enacting its identity theft statute. The state acknowledged the increase in the incidence of identity theft, the rising financial impact of identity theft on society, and the impact on the victims.[17] The legislature also referenced the necessary power of the state to regulate matters affecting the health, safety, and welfare of its citizens. In other words, the state announced that in the case of identity theft, it was relying on its "police power" to regulate the growing crime problem. Illinois broadly defined the crime of identity theft to include the circumstance of a person knowingly using any personal identifying information of another to commit a fraud. Aggravated identity theft, that is, a case of identity theft committed against the more vulnerable members of society, carries enhanced penalties.

Laws are often created to protect the more vulnerable members of our society. Often this special protection is aimed at protecting children and/or the elderly, those least able to protect themselves. Illinois took a creative and noble approach in the creation of its identity theft statute by including a provision regarding aggravated identity theft intended to protect disabled individuals and individuals over sixty years of age.[18] A person who commits an aggravated identity theft faces at least a class 4 felony.[19] Legislatures and courts have an obligation and a responsibility to look out for the interests of the more vulnerable members of society. And in this ever more technologically complex society, where criminals can run scams on victims over the Internet, phone, or otherwise, people over the age of sixty and disabled individu-

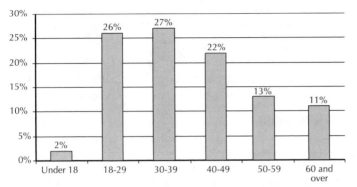

FIGURE 5. Identity Theft by Victim Age
Data represent total identity theft complaints to the Consumer Sentinel database where a victim age was given (94%).

als (who may both be less technologically adept) deserve special protection from identity theft. In fact, the statute may deter a criminal from targeting one group in favor of another. The realization, codified in statute in Illinois, that not only is the size of the crime important but also the status of the victim represents a novel but important way of thinking about identity theft and how it should be punished.

California's, Florida's, and Illinois' identity theft statutes all contain valuable provisions. Each contains a new wrinkle or twist. Each views identity theft differently than the others and in a slightly unique way. While each of these state statutes represents a step forward in identity theft law, the Washington State statute regarding identity theft is a step even beyond these. The Washington statute is one of the most comprehensive and innovative of all state statutes regarding identity theft.

Washington Statutory Law Regarding Identity Theft

Like Florida and Illinois, Washington State also passed a statute addressing identity theft in 1999, in the wake of the 1998 federal statute. While some states have many degrees of identity theft defined as misdemeanors and/or many levels of felony, Washington classifies all identity theft as felonies. And there are three levels of felony, depending on the value of property involved in the fraud. Washington penalizes any violations of its identity theft statute as either a class C or class B felony:

> Violation of this section when the accused or an accomplice uses the victim's means of identification or financial information and obtains an aggregate total of credit, money, goods, services, or anything else of value in excess of one thousand five hundred dollars in value shall constitute identity theft in the first degree. Identity theft in the first degree is a class B felony. . . . Violation of this section when the accused or an accomplice uses the victim's means of identification or financial information and obtains an aggregate total of credit, money, goods, services, or anything else of value that is less than one thousand five hundred dollars in value shall constitute identity theft in the second degree. Identity theft in the second degree is a class C felony.[20]

Class C felonies in Washington are punishable by imprisonment for up to five years, or a $10,000 fine, or both.[21] Class B felonies in Washington are punishable by imprisonment for up to ten years or a fine of up to $20,000, or both the fine and imprisonment.[22] Class A felonies in Washington are punishable by life imprisonment or a fine of $50,000 or both.[23] The Washington State statute contains many provisions that merit attention. The Illinois legislature cited many pubic policy reasons necessitating an identity theft statute. The Washington legislature cited similar public policy rationale. However, the Washington legislature emphasized the privacy violation of identity theft, and clearly stated its intent to punish those who commit the crime.[24]

The Washington statute also recognizes that while identity theft is an invasion of the privacy of an individual and a crime deserving of punishment in its own right, it is also frequently part and parcel of a larger criminal enterprise. The statute broadly prohibits the wrongful use of any identification of another to further any other crime:

No person may knowingly obtain, possess, use, or transfer a means of identification or financial information of another person, living or dead, with the intent to commit, or to aid or abet, any crime.[25]

This recognition of the somewhat dual nature of identity theft as both a stand-alone and a component crime is an important acknowledgment and an important step forward.

Most states with identity theft statutes only codify the crime of identity theft and do not address civil liability. The Washington statute does both. There is recognition of and an attempt to address civil liability of identity criminals. A criminal convicted under Washington's criminal identity theft statute is automatically civilly liable for at least $500. Actual liability may be an amount equal to the actual damages plus the costs necessary to fix the damage done by the criminal.[26] As with many civil judgments, the possibility of actually collecting the judgment may not be great. The recognition that the criminal is responsible for not only the real cost of the money stolen but also the costs of repairing a badly damaged financial and credit history may help victims achieve the closure that so often eludes them.

Most state statutes regarding identity theft do not address jurisdiction. The proper court in which to bring criminal and or civil action against the perpetrator is often unclear. Jurisdiction of an identity theft crime is an important issue. If an identity thief commits a crime over the computer and Internet it is often unclear where exactly the crime occurred and where justice should be pursued. The Washington statute establishes jurisdiction where the victim resides, thus making access to justice easier for the victim. The statute allows for jurisdiction in "any locality where the person whose means of identification or financial information was appropriated resides, or in which any part of the offense took place."[27] Reducing the nonmonetary costs to individuals in the pursuit of justice or restitution should work to increase not only the rate of identity theft complaints but also the willingness of prosecutors to aggressively pursue cases.

Unintended consequences of laws can bring injustice and absurdity, but are consequences often not foreseeable by even the most prescient legislator, prosecutor or judge. The Washington State legislature was able to foresee one unintended possibility, that identity theft laws might ensnare underage individuals who obtain false identifications for the purpose of getting into establishments that serve alcohol. The Washington legislature specifically excluded this group from liability under the identity theft law. Underage drinkers were not intended to be covered by the identity theft law and statutory penalties.[28]

As with other state identity theft statutes, such as Florida's, Washington's specifically grants courts authority to issue orders as necessary to correct public records of the identity theft victim. Factual findings of innocence and other judicial declarations may be issued to help the victim recover from the lingering effects of the crime committed against him or her. The statute also gives identity theft victims other governmental assistance and tools with which to repair damage done by identity thieves.

Victims and businesses are often at odds in identity theft cases. Businesses have duties to protect the privacy of their customers' sensitive information. When a business unwittingly does business with an identity thief, it should be responsible for its error. Businesses are contacted frequently with requests from victims for information. These requests can be for copies of purchase records, charge receipts with fraudulent signatures, or forged checks that can provide fraudulent account numbers and other data. These victims need this type of information about the fraud committed using their identity to assist them in clearing their name with banks and creditors and reestablishing their credit ratings. Citing privacy laws, businesses typically refuse to give up the information to the victim. Often adding insult to injury and delaying or destroying any chance for the victim to seek and gain punishment for the crime and restitution, businesses will use the very laws that the identity thief has broken to thwart the victim in his or her quest for justice.

The drafters of the Washington statute, cognizant of this very problem, addressed the issue in the identity theft statute. The Washington provision requires that businesses, upon appropriate written request from an identity theft victim, provide the requested documents to the victim.[29] This discovery provision tremendously helps victims of identity theft to gain the information necessary to cause prosecutors to criminally charge identity thieves and to allow the victims to pursue civil action. The provision certainly also helps victims to obtain the information necessary to repair their credit and financial identities. A business may still be able to deny the request of a victim, but it must have a good faith legal reason to deny the request. That decision is also a possible cause for legal action and review by the judicial system.

The Washington state legislature also made a violation of the identity theft statute a violation of the Consumer Protection Act, giving victims yet more legal tools to use to combat identity thieves and get the information necessary to restore their credit and financial lives.[30] A successful suit under the Consumer Protection Act may net the plaintiff an award of treble damages up to $10,000, attorney fees, and costs. Again, the statute recognizes that identity theft is a new type of crime that contains many elements of older crimes. As such, identity theft needs to be addressed in new ways, but that can also include the use of existing legal tools in innovative ways.

The Washington theft statute contains one more notable provision:

> Within thirty days of receipt of proof of the consumer's identification and a copy of a filed police report evidencing the consumer's claim to be a victim of a violation of RCW 9.35.020, a consumer reporting agency shall permanently block reporting any information the consumer identifies on his or her consumer report as a result of a violation of RCW 9.35.020, so that the information cannot be reported.
>
> The consumer reporting agency shall promptly notify the furnisher of the information that a police report has been filed, that a block has been requested, and the effective date of the block.[31]

Generally through the above provision, consumer reporting agencies may be required to block identity theft-related information if requested by the identity theft victim. A consumer reporting agency may decline to block the information, if the declination is in good faith and for a reason provided by the statute.

Published Cases of Identity Theft from Washington

Because identity theft is a relatively new form of crime, there is only one published court opinion involving identity theft in Washington, *State v. Baldwin*.[32] The facts according to the court are as follows:

> Baldwin, representing herself as the victim, Kaytie Allshouse, purchased a house, forging Allshouse's name on two deeds of trust. The first deed of trust secured the interest of an institutional lender . . . the second . . . deed was in favor of the sellers. . . . The deeds secured payment of $45,500, and $6,500, respectively. Two months later, Baldwin rented a mailbox at the Mail Room, a mailbox-rental outlet in Everett. Baldwin presented herself as yet another person, Monica Schultz, and produced a Washington driver's license bearing that name. She signed Schultz's name to the mailbox application and began receiving mail in at least 15 names. Baldwin later rented a mailbox . . . at Cascade Storage, another mailbox-rental outlet. . . . Meanwhile, a United States postal inspector acting on a complaint placed a 30-day mail cover on the Cascade Storage box address. Under a mail cover, all mail to a specific address is recorded by postmark, addressee, sender, and class of mail. The mail cover revealed mail in numerous names being sent to the rented box. The inspector then contacted a detective for the Snohomish County Sheriff's Office responsible for investigating financial crimes. The detective traced the telephone number listed on the Cascade Storage rental paperwork to Baldwin. His suspicions that Baldwin had stolen . . . identity were confirmed when Cascade Storage manager . . . picked Baldwin's picture out of a photomontage. . . . A search of the Granite Falls property [of Baldwin] yielded a wallet containing a Washington driver's license in the name of 'Kaytie Allshouse' bearing Baldwin's picture, and two VISA cards, also in the name of 'Kaytie Allshouse.'[33]

Baldwin was charged with and convicted of multiple counts of identity theft and forgery. Jeanne Baldwin received an exceptional sentence of 36 months, as the court found that the amount of economic harm was "greater than usual" and that the crime was one of a "high degree of sophistication."[34] The court not only upheld the convictions on all counts but the exceptional sentence as well.[35] The Baldwin case provides an excellent example of a sophisticated identity theft scheme, how law enforcement was able to figure out that scheme, and illustrates when an exceptional sentence may be appropriate under the Washington State statute.

Conclusion: A Model State Identity Theft Statute

After looking at the California, Florida, Illinois, and Washington identity theft statutes, there are a number of observations that can be made. There is clearly no such uniform state law with different states choosing different means of addressing the problem. The fact that there is no uniform state law regarding identity theft is both a good and a bad thing. Not having a uniform state law across all fifty states allows each state to adopt different and creative approaches to identity theft. Over time the statutory provisions that work well in one state can diffuse horizontally and other states can choose to model those laws or provisions that have proven effective or useful. Each of the states examined above has created a statute that contains this type of provision.

California's identity theft statute contains provisions that all states would do well to incorporate. Specifically, the provisions that require law enforcement to take a police report regarding identity theft and to begin an investigation would benefit victims of identity theft in all states. Also, the provision that allows a victim to petition a court for a factual finding of innocence would be a useful tool nationally. Florida's identity theft statutes also employ well the principle of proportionality, as the punishment prescribed for different violations fits the crime defined. Illinois' identity theft statute provides additional protections for the disabled and those over sixty years of age. It makes identity theft committed against these groups an aggravated identity theft. The principle of proportionality exemplified by the Florida statute and the Illinois statute as well should be used as a model when other states seek to create or refine their identity theft statutes.

Washington's identity theft statute is noteworthy for a number of reasons. It gives victims a tool with which to obtain records from businesses regarding the identity theft, so the victim can begin to repair the damage done. A criminal violation in Washington automatically establishes civil liability, and a violation of the identity theft statute is also a violation of the Consumer Protection Act. Washington's provision allowing for a block of information appearing as a result of identity theft should also be modeled, as might its attempts to limit unintended consequences, which makes it clear that the legislature did not intend that the statute apply to underage drinkers who misused identification for that purpose. A uniform identity theft statute would be easier to employ and understand, and if it incorporated the best provisions of the statutes highlighted in this conclusion, would better further justice. As the law stands now, an individual must closely examine his or her state's identity theft statute to learn what protections and remedies, if any, are afforded by particular state law.

There is every indication that identity theft rates continue to increase, and the costs, both direct and indirect, will rise as a result. As the federal government finds itself increasingly involved in international issues and combating international terrorism, it will continue to devolve more responsibility onto states. Clearly, states are going to have to arrive at effective means of combating the problem. The statute in Washington provides what is probably the clearest road map for thinking about a model identity theft statute, but even that is incomplete.

CHAPTER 6

Case Studies

The Importance of Case Studies

Different case studies of identity theft can provide unique insights into the complexity of the problem and are illustrative of many of the issues raised throughout this book. Although the FTC keeps statistics of the numbers of cases of identity theft reported, there presently is no comprehensive database on enforcement results under the federal or collective states' identity theft statutes.[1] "The crime of identity theft is not specifically recorded as an offense category in the FBI's Uniform Crime Reporting Program."[2] However, it is possible to find information on some specific examples of cases of identity theft for purposes of illustration and discussion. As international terrorism is facilitated by identity theft, identity fraud, and credit card fraud, it is enlightening to examine a particular case of international terrorism, that of Ahmed Ressam, in which identity theft played a key role.[3] Through examining Ressam's case and the role that identity fraud played, we can better understand terrorists' and identity thieves' strategies and tactics and can learn what risky transactions or activities to avoid, and maybe how to better prevent not only terrorism, but identity theft as well.

The Ressam case is certainly an important example of identity theft because it was part of an international terrorism plot. It is not, however, necessarily typical of most cases of identity theft. While there are numerous examples of international identity theft, much of the problem occurs within the United States. It is useful to examine some more "garden variety" incidents of identity theft that have occurred domestically. Specifically through the examination of some cases in California, Florida, and Washington, we can arrive at a better understanding of the wide variety of tactics used by identity thieves and can see how some cases were handled under the law.

One of the most useful possible case studies is an examination of the identity theft case of Adelaide Andrews. This case is important and useful to review for a number of reasons. First, the identity theft case of Ms. Andrews is the only recent fact pattern of identity theft to make it to the United States Supreme Court. That, in and of itself, makes the case both unique and interesting. Second, Ms. Andrews' case illustrates well how some cases of identity theft can turn on very narrow points of fact and of law. Third is the fact that Ms. Andrews' case is a common fact pattern of identity theft. As such, we can use it to identify and learn about common but significant dangers to avoid. Finally, Ms. Andrews' case of identity theft gives us the chance to explore issues of legal liability in such cases.

The last case study presented will examine one of the largest ever alleged cases of identity theft in the United

States. This case study highlights once again the possible international character of identity theft and how difficult globalization of identity theft and the international black market for stolen credit card numbers makes investigation and prosecution. Since the horrific terrorist attacks of September 11, 2001, the nation's law enforcement priority has shifted to counterterrorism. Accordingly, it makes sense to begin our discussion with the Ahmed Ressam international terrorism case.

Identity Theft and International Terrorism

Ahmed Ressam, now a convicted Al Qaeda-trained terrorist, used identity theft as an integral part of a plot to further that terrorist group's objectives. He almost successfully carried out a plot to explode a bomb at Los Angeles International Airport. Fortunately for all, Ressam was apprehended shortly after he crossed the border from Canada into the United States in Washington State. Ressam was eventually convicted of nine counts related to transporting explosives into the United States with the intent to commit a terrorist act. Facing up to 130 years in prison, Ressam began cooperating with law enforcement after his conviction in the hopes of receiving a more lenient sentence.[4] Scheduled to be sentenced in March 2003 for his role in the terrorism plot, Ressam may receive as little as 27 years in prison because of his cooperation with federal authorities.[5] That sentencing has now been delayed indefinitely to allow Ressam to continue to testify against other suspected terrorists.

On July 3, 2001, Ahmed Ressam testified in federal court against an associate of his, Mokhtar Haouari, who was accused of participating in terrorist activities. Ressam's courtroom testimony unveiled the inner workings of the complicated Al Qaeda international terrorist organization and the role of its Taliban sponsors. Ressam's testimony contributed to Haouari's conviction on federal charges including fake identification and other material to others involved in the terrorism plot. Haouari was sentenced to 24 years in prison.[6]

The story of Ahmed Ressam and his criminal activities begins much earlier than that particular court appearance. Much of his early life is unclear but he was born in Algeria and graduated from high school there in or about 1988. He worked with his father in a coffee shop until 1992, when he left Algeria for France to look for work. Ressam entered France illegally, and from about 1992 until 1994 worked in Corsica picking grapes and oranges at a vineyard and as a painter at a tourist resort. In 1994, he left France for Canada to find better employment.

Ressam used a fake French passport to attempt to enter Canada. When he arrived at Montreal, however, immigration stopped him, and he admitted to having a false passport. Ressam concocted a story about his being a victim of political oppression and formally requested asylum in Canada. Canadian officials let Ressam stay pending investigation of his asylum claim. He lived in Montreal from 1994 until 1998—alone for a while, and then with friends Labsi Mustafa, Boumezbeur Adel, and Atmani Said. During that four-year period, Ressam lived on welfare provided by the Canadian government and stole from tourists. When asked to clarify what he meant by committing "theft," Ressam testified:

> I used to steal [from] tourists, rob tourists. I used to go to hotels and find their suitcases and steal them. . . . I used to take the money, keep the money, and if there are passports, I would sell them, and if there are Visa credit cards, I would use them up, and if there were any traveler's checks, I would use them or sell them.[7]

Ressam admitted to committing this type of crime 30 to 40 times, being arrested 4 times, and only once being convicted and fined, but never sent to prison. He testified that it was in 1994, after he arrived in Canada, that he first met Haouri. Ressam and Haouri talked about opening bank accounts with probable stolen checks, and between 1994 and 1998, they sold stolen passports together. Ressam admitted to providing Haouri with identity papers including Social Security cards, driver's licenses, and bank cards. These had all been stolen by his friend Mustafa. As compensation, Ressam received $60 for the identity documents. In 1997, Ressam sent his Canadian passport to Haouri in exchange for $110, in part because Ressam wanted a "better passport."

Ressam had heard about training camps in Afghanistan from his friends, who encouraged him to go. Ressam admitted to having an interest in joining jihad in Algeria. He bought a ticket to travel from Montreal to Karachi using false identity papers. Once in Pakistan, he contacted Abu Zubeida, who was in charge of the terrorist training camps in Afghanistan. Ressam conceded that Abu Zubeida was an alias, but insisted that he did not know the man's true name. Ressam claimed that all who attended the training camps used aliases. Ressam's alias was "Nabil." Zubeida sent Ressam to an Afghan training camp called Khalden. At any given time, there were between 50 and 100 people attending the camp. Representatives of many nationalities were present, including people from Jordan, Algeria, Yemen, Saudi Arabia, Sweden, Germany, France, Turkey, and Chechnya. Ressam spent between five and six months in the terrorist training camps and received instruction on how to use all types of guns and a rocket propelled grenade launcher. The Taliban provided the ammunition to the training camp. Ressam trained in how to use explosives and how to make TNT and C4, two particularly dangerous explosives.

Ressam learned sabotage techniques and how to "blow up the infrastructure of a country." He received training in urban warfare and how to stalk and assassinate a very important and well-protected person. He received further training in explosives, and when asked about how he was to use them, Ressam stated "First . . . surveil a place. When you go to a place you would wear clothing that would not bring suspicion to yourself, you would wear clothing that tourists wear. You would observe or you would take pictures."[8] Ressam testified to wanting to attack the United States before the year 2000, and that he and others discussed bombing an airport at one point. Before leaving Afghanistan, Ressam saw Zubeida one more time. Zubeida requested that Ressam send him original false passports for others to use to carry out operations in the United States. Ressam brought back to Canada $12,000, instructions on how to make explosives, and some chemicals.

A mutual friend reacquainted Ressam with Haouri, because Ressam needed a Visa card. Haouri agreed to allow Ressam to state that he was working at Haouri's store so that Ressam could get the card. Haouri filled out the credit card application for Ressam, stating Ressam's name as Benny Noris, the alias that Ressam was using at the time, and the alias Ressam would use to enter the United States. Haouri and others used to get Visa card numbers and names of people from restaurants or stores, and Ressam would make counterfeit credit cards with the good numbers. Later, Haouri, Ressam, and another individual discussed the prospect of Ressam opening a business for them. The business would be a front set up in order to obtain Visa card numbers from customers.

In February of 1999, Ressam began preparation to bomb a target in the United States. When asked about how he prepared, Ressam stated, "First I put my papers in order, my documents . . . my bank card, driver's license, and insurance card . . . in the name of Benny Noris." Ressam obtained another set of fake identification documents with the alias Mario Roig, possibly for use in escaping after he completed the bombing. Because some of the accomplices he had chosen could not get out of Europe, Ressam decided to proceed with the plan to bomb Los Angeles International Airport himself. He picked the airport as a target "because an airport is sensitive politically and economically."

Ressam had planned to scout the airport before carrying out his plan: "I will put the cart in a place that is not suspicious and then I will observe the reaction of security, how long it took them to observe it." The first time, he planned to do this without explosives; the second time, he planned to use explosives. Ressam then put his plan into action, crossing from Canada into the United States:

> On December 14, 1999, at approximately 6:00 p.m., an individual identifying himself as "Benni Antoine Noris" entered the United States at Port Angeles, Washington, on the ferryboat "Coho" from Victoria, British Columbia, Canada. Noris was driving a Chrysler 300, British Columbia license plate number ANF304, which he rented in Vancouver, BC. Noris' vehicle was the last car off the ferry. U.S. Customs Inspectors performed a secondary Customs examination of the car and requested Noris get out of the vehicle, but initially he was uncooperative.
>
> Benni Antoine Noris filled out a CF 6059B Customs Baggage Declaration Form which he presented to U.S. Customs Inspector Diana Dean. The form listed his name as Benni Noris with a date of birth of May 9, 1971. In addition, Noris presented a Costco card with the name of Benni Noris and his photograph to another U.S. Customs Inspector. Customs Inspectors later discovered in the vehicle a Canadian Passport, #VE537438, in the name of Benni Antoine Noris, date of birth May 9, 1971; a Quebec driver's license, #PCC305CUW, in the name of Mario Roig, date of birth May 9, 1971. Additionally, U.S. Customs Inspectors discovered at least eight (8) credit cards in the name Benni Noris.[9]

Customs officials proceeded to inspect the rest of Ressam's car and discovered explosives hidden in the vehicle. At about the same time Ressam decided to attempt an escape and fled on foot. He was apprehended after a short chase. He was tried and convicted on nine counts related to international terrorism.

Ressam was simply using the basic techniques of identity theft. These were techniques that he had used many times previously throughout his life. He had entered France illegally using false identification at a very young age, he had attempted to enter Canada illegally using a false passport, and he had lived in Canada by victimizing the identities of others. He had even managed to travel back and forth between Canada and Pakistan using stolen and assumed identities. Finally he had attempted to enter the United States using fraudulent identification.

The case of Ahmed Ressam is certainly frightening because of the scope of the ultimate crime planned. We have
all become much more aware of the possibility of terrorist
acts in our country. While that is indeed frightening, what is
of equal concern is the ease with which Ressam was able to
carry out his plan. If not for a single decision at the border
north of Seattle, Ressam, disguised as Benni Noris, would
have been able to carry out his plot and likely escape using
yet another false identity. He had lived and worked for years
under false, assumed, and stolen names and had gotten
away with it very handily. It is clear not only that identity
theft needs to be treated much more seriously here as well
as abroad but also that cooperation between nations is
going to be essential in reversing the tide of international
identity theft.

Cases of Identity Theft from California

Several interesting cases of identity theft have arisen in
California in recent years. In one case, a very bold individual
allegedly stole the identities of 28 people. A significant feat
in itself, the thief did not stop there. He proceeded to use
those 28 stolen identities to submit 28 false federal income
tax returns. Filing some of the forms through the U.S. postal
system and some electronically over the Internet, the thief
requested income tax refunds averaging approximately
$50,000 for each return filed.[10]

Nnamdi Opara was arrested for allegedly trying to commit a major fraud against the United States through identity
theft. Besides trying to defraud the United States, Opara
also allegedly unlawfully obtained an American Express
card number belonging to Ted Danson, the television star of
Cheers and *Becker* fame, and used that card to order a digital
camera. He had requested that the camera be delivered to a
mailbox that he controlled. As a result of all charges, Opara
faces more than 560 years in prison and a fine of
$14,000,000. Most criminals who commit identity theft

and related crimes commit simple credit card fraud and face lesser but significant penalties. The penalties in this particular case are so large because the majority of the alleged crimes were committed against the government of the United States. Smarter criminals also avoid high profile names like Ted Danson, as high profile individuals may be more likely to generate police and or media investigations, which of course these criminals want to avoid.

As already noted, identity theft often is committed in furtherance of or in addition to other crimes. This next case illustrates that sometimes identity theft is ancillary to a horrific crime. Supawan Veerapol, a Thai national, was found guilty of one count of involuntary servitude and three counts of harboring undocumented Thai women at her home. Ms. Veerapol was sentenced to 97 months in prison for holding several women in her home against their will.[11] In addition to being held against their will, the Thai women were forced to work in the house, and Veerapol threatened their families if the women tried to leave. While holding the Thai women in slavery, Ms. Veerapol used the identities of two of her victims to open credit card accounts. She used these fraudulent accounts to order and receive more than $80,000 worth of property. Ms. Veerapol was eventually convicted of six counts of mail fraud related to the identity theft. It is tragic and sad that cases of slavery can still occur in the United States or anywhere in the world these days. While cases of modern slavery are rare, identity theft in conjunction with credit card fraud is common, and often part and parcel of other crimes, even the most heinous. The theft of the identities of her victims was not the major motive behind the underlying crimes of Ms. Veerapol. That she was so easily able to steal the identities of individuals, some of whom were not even in the country legally, and translate that theft into thousands of dollars in ill-gotten gain points to the ease with which identity theft can occur.

Often, perpetrators of identity theft obtain private, sensitive, personal identifying information in the ordinary course of business or at their place of employment. Think about traveling across the country today and all of the steps necessary to complete the journey. A traveler has to book air or other transportation, purchase meals, and secure lodging. Numerous transactions are necessary, and often a credit card to carry them out. Many businesses and their employees have access to a large volume of credit card numbers and information, and they may store that information in their in-house databases. The next case study illustrates how employees can abuse their positions to obtain credit card information and commit identity theft and fraudulent transactions.

A customer service representative employed at a car rental agency at the Sacramento International Airport, Charles Timothy, stole identity information in the course of his employment.[12] Timothy and two others, Oliver Alaefule and Ifeany Onwuazo, then used that stolen personal identifying information to apply for credit cards. These individuals obtained more than twenty different mailboxes at numerous private mailbox centers in the Sacramento area, to which they had the illegally obtained credit cards sent. This identity theft scheme involved over $500,000. Credit is not impossible to avoid but it has become a larger and more frequent part of the daily lives of many Americans. This case should serve to give pause to anyone thinking about using credit cards even in the normal course of business. Certainly it is always potentially dangerous to give out credit or other sensitive information when making travel arrangements or transacting business of any kind. Even if the company with which you are dealing is reputable, the person behind the counter may not be.

Cases of Identity Theft from Florida

Most people think that going out to dinner is an innocent and relatively safe activity and give the possibility of identity theft little thought. However, restaurants often conduct business on a large scale and in large volume, with customers often paying their bills with credit cards for convenience, tax purposes, or for other reasons. Employees of the restaurants, even those not in managerial positions are able to access and steal the sensitive identifying information of the customer. As we know, once they have that information, they can, as with the car rental employees above, easily use it to commit identity theft and related fraud. Even more sinisterly, computer hackers could tap into an innocent restaurant or other business, access a legitimate database, and steal the information necessary to commit identity theft.

The following case illustrates the danger of trusting credit card information to even an upstanding restaurant with innocent employees. David Prouty and Nicole Conde were indicted on federal charges relating to their alleged illegal conduct of tapping into computer networks of restaurants throughout Florida.[13] In a massive operation, the pair allegedly tapped into hundreds of computer databases. By the time they were eventually caught, they had allegedly used the illegally obtained credit card account numbers of more than 12,000 customers. Worse still, they had distributed some of the stolen numbers widely over the Internet. The pair had allegedly created and used a front company, called Mobli Oli Adms, Inc., to further and conceal their illegal conduct. Once they had established the front company, they were able to run their stolen account numbers, charging the accounts for goods and services never received. Account numbers from several major credit card carriers were taken, including Visa and American Express. American Express alone estimated losses to be more than $7,000,000. As a result of their crimes, each defendant faces up to ten years in prison.

Not all cases of identity theft are of the scale of Prouty and Conde. In some cases, the crime is committed for reasons other than the obvious financial gain of credit card fraud. Edward Chwojko, for instance, pled guilty on charges that he possessed false identification documents that he intended to use to defraud the United States in violation of Title 18, United States Code, section 1028(a)(4).[14] Chwojko and his wife owned and operated cleaning companies,

Ankas Cleaning Service and Florida Hotel Cleaning Service, in Key West, Florida. Chwojko habitually employed illegal aliens of eastern European descent and needed documents to support their ability to work in the United States. He used both false Social Security numbers and real Social Security numbers stolen from other individuals. Far from a beneficent employer, Chwojko charged the illegal aliens between $150 and $250 for the bogus Social Security cards and INS Form I-94 Departure Record. Fortunately, Chwojko apparently kept a record of payment and Social Security numbers assigned, making prosecution much easier.

On April 19, 2001, a federal grand jury sitting in Miami returned a seven-count credit card fraud and false identification card indictment against Julio Arjona.[15] Allegedly, Arjona used credit card skimmers—small hand-held devices that read magnetic strips—to steal credit card numbers, and then he manufactured credit cards using those numbers. Arjona allegedly stole credit card numbers of Visa, American Express, and MasterCard credit cards and manufactured false Florida driver's licenses for use with them. Law enforcement authorities executed two search warrants on Arjona's home and found 21 credit card skimmers and equipment to manufacture more of the devices. Arjona faced a maximum imprisonment term of fifteen years if convicted on these charges.

These cases from Florida present a wide array of the types of identity theft and the underlying reasons why it is committed. From cases involving international trafficking in human beings to high-tech tapping of computer databases, the criminals put their crime to various nefarious uses. What links all of these crimes and criminals are the relative ease with which they were able to commit their crimes and the amounts of money involved. In most instances we have indeed become blasé about providing credit cards to businesses, trusting that those transactions are secure. That they may not be is certainly a disturbing thought.

Cases of Identity Theft from Washington

Believe it or not, there was even a case of identity theft in Washington State that involved a university professor of philosophy and ethics—as the perpetrator! James Cadello, a reputable academic, pled guilty to one count of identity fraud on April 25, 2000.[16] Cadello executed a fairly complex scheme. He acquired identification documents in names other than his own. Once he had those documents, he was able to submit false applications for Social Security cards for nonexistent children by representing himself as the parent. He also obtained state identification documents in the names of the nonexistent children. "According to court papers, more than 40 identification documents in 14 different names were seized by federal agents in a February 4, 2000, search of his home in Ellensburg."[17] What makes this scheme most interesting is that the documents obtained from the government would be official documents. That is, the Social Security numbers would be valid as far as the SSA would know. Valid documents are much more valuable than documents that have been stolen because the latter can trip up a thief when reported.

Another Washington identity thief, Jerome Vassar, pled guilty to two counts of bank fraud and one count of identity theft.[18] Vassar and an accomplice used the name, birth date, Social Security number, and savings account number of the identity theft victim to transfer $15,000 from the victim's bank account to a newly created E-Trade bank account. Vassar also obtained a bank account number belonging to the United Way of King County and created a completely bogus check in the amount of $99,979.35 using the account number and a home computer.

Vassar opened an account with the Janus investment company and deposited the fraudulently created check. Once in a legitimate account controlled by him, he could then draw checks on the Janus account. The first check, made payable to the victim in the amount of $49,990, was mailed from Janus to an address that Vassar could access. Vassar then cashed the check at a Moneymart Store in Seattle using a fake Washington State driver's license with the victim's name and birth date. Vassar then drew a second check from the Janus account in the amount of $40,000. With the help of a juvenile accomplice, he deposited the second check into a savings account at the Bank of America, which was created jointly in the name of the juvenile and the identity theft victim. Vassar then had the juvenile withdraw about $33,000 in cash from that account and make out two cashier's checks issued to Vassar.

This scheme was a highly convoluted attempt to steal large sums of money by using the identity of another. Despite the convoluted trail leading to the money, Vassar was caught and prosecuted in Washington State. He faces a maximum of 30 years in prison and a $1,000,000 fine on each bank fraud charge, and a maximum of up to 15 years in prison and a fine of $250,000 on the identity theft charge.

The third Washington thief is Michael Trollinger, who pled guilty to a litany of charges including possession of a counterfeit postal key, possession of stolen mail, and identity theft; John Heckendorn, his accomplice, pled guilty to charges of escape, conspiracy to possess stolen mail, possession of counterfeit postal keys, possession of false identification documents, and production of false identification documents.[19] After Trollinger was arrested, law enforcement conducted a search of his hotel room and recovered stolen mail and two counterfeit Washington State driver's licenses with photographs of Trollinger and names and addresses of mail theft victims.

Trollinger was released from custody and then apprehended a short time later after he tried to use counterfeit U.S. postal keys to access a mailbox at an apartment complex. A short time later, Trollinger's fingerprints were found on a counterfeit check cashed at a Wells Fargo bank. The check was cashed using an identity theft victim's information. Law enforcement then executed another search warrant on Trollinger's residence in Seattle and discovered more stolen mail, stolen identity information, a counterfeit U.S. Postal Service lock and counterfeit Postal Service keys, as well as other evidence of crimes including identity theft.

Heckendorn, Trollinger's accomplice, had escaped from a halfway house where he had been confined pursuant to a conviction for federal bank fraud in late 2000. Heckendorn had shared with Trollinger the hotel room where stolen mail and other evidence were discovered. Heckendorn was arrested at a motel in Marysville, Washington, and law enforcement then discovered more stolen mail, another counterfeit Postal Service lock and keys, and counterfeit Washington State driver's licenses containing Heckendorn's photograph, but names and addresses of victims of mail and identity theft. Police also recovered counterfeit checks and other significant evidence. Trollinger and Heckendorn admitted that they were each responsible for the theft of at least $70,000 and possibly more than $100,000. Under federal statutes and the Washington law, they each faced five years in prison for possession of stolen mail, ten years in prison for possession of counterfeit postal keys, and fifteen years in prison for identity theft and possession or production of false documents.

These cases from Washington present yet more wrinkles in the identity theft picture. From quick, almost snatch-and-grab affairs to very complex schemes to hide the crimes, identity thieves are constantly working to secure the necessary information to defraud victims and the government.

The Andrews Case of Identity Theft

Adelaide Andrews was a victim of identity theft, and her case made it all the way to the Supreme Court of the United States, the only identity theft case that has so far made it to that level.[20] Adelaide's case was plainly one of identity theft, but the legal issues presented to and decided by the Supreme Court did not directly address identity theft. However, examining the fact pattern of the Adelaide Andrews case is quite enlightening and leads to further observations regarding identity theft.

> On June 17, 1993, Adelaide Andrews visited a radiologist's office in Santa Monica, California. She filled out a new patient form listing certain basic information, including her name, birth date, and Social Security number. Andrews handed the form to the office receptionist, one Andrea Andrews (the impostor), who copied the information and thereafter moved to Las Vegas, Nevada. Once there, the impostor attempted on numerous occasions to open credit accounts using Andrews' Social Security number and her own last name and address.
>
> On four of those occasions, the company from which the impostor sought credit requested a report from TRW. Each time, TRW's computers registered a match between Andrew's Social Security number, last name, and first initial and therefore responded by furnishing her file. TRW thus disclosed Andrews' credit history at the impostor's request to a bank on July 25, 1994; to a cable television company on September 27, 1994; to a department store on October 28, 1994; and to another credit provider on January 3, 1995. All recipients but the cable company rejected the impostor's application for credit.
>
> Andrews did not learn of these disclosures until May 31, 1995, when she sought to refinance her home mortgage and in the process received a copy of her credit report reflecting the impostor's activity. Andrews concedes that TRW promptly corrected her file upon learning of its mistake. She alleges, however, that the blemishes on her report not only caused her inconvenience and emotional distress, they also forced her to abandon her refinancing efforts and settle for an alternative line of credit on less favorable terms.[21]

Andrews sued TRW claiming that TRW violated the Fair Credit Reporting Act by failing to verify that she, and not the impostor, was involved in the transactions. TRW countered that the statute of limitations had expired on the July 25 and September 27 disclosures. The main issue considered by the Supreme Court in this case was when the two-year statute of limitations had begun and, if so, if it had expired. The Supreme Court held that the specific two-year statute of limitations in this case applied and that it had expired, even

though Andrews had not had actual knowledge of the disclosures until May 1995. She did not actually file suit until
October 1996, more than two years after the disclosures.
Her lack of knowledge of the wrongful disclosures, alone,
did not toll the statute of limitations.

The Andrews case presents many useful illustrations.
First, the fact pattern itself is a typical identity theft fact pattern, which is still a problem today. An impostor at a place
of business, a doctor's office, misappropriated a patient's
private information, which we all provide and usually without a second thought. The impostor then used that information, unbeknownst to the victim, to open and abuse credit
accounts, and damaged the victim's credit rating. The victim did not find out about the perpetrator's actions until
after more than a year had passed.

This fact pattern occurred before federal law and many
state laws specifically against identity theft had been
passed. Clearly Andrews was victimized, her privacy terribly invaded, and her life seriously inconvenienced. Had
the crimes occurred after the passage of those laws, the out-
come of the case might have been different. The identity of
the victims in this case seems clear. There remains, however, a question of who was responsible for the identity
theft in the Andrews case.

The most obviously responsible party is the impostor, the
thief. The impostor faces federal and state criminal and extensive civil liability. Practically speaking, the impostor will
most likely go to jail for many years. Civil liability is much
more challenging given that the perpetrators of identity
theft, like other criminals, often have no recoverable assets
and may be practically immune from civil damages. There
are other possible responsible parties in the Andrews case.

TRW, sued by Andrews, certainly had responsibilities to
her. TRW will not be held criminally liable as long as it acted
in good faith and generally reasonably. There may be a different story with civil liability, however. TRW's actions may not
have risen to criminal liability, but may have been civilly neg-
ligent in operating its computers and storing and securing

sensitive information. TRW could possibly be liable for gross negligence or possibly intentional torts but, as always, liability depends on the particular facts, circumstances, and laws of each case.[22]

Remember, the impostor in the Andrews case worked at a medical doctor's office. If the impostor had a criminal record involving crimes of dishonesty and the employer did not check the employees' or potential employees' criminal history and hired them anyway, the employer may be civilly liable for negligently hiring the impostor. Also, if a place of business regularly handles sensitive information and does not have reasonable safeguards to protect that sensitive information, the business could be liable for the unauthorized disclosure. Everyone that handles the sensitive information in the chain of the information flow has some responsibility for the information, and could be legally liable for failing to reasonably safeguard it.

Largest Alleged Case of Identity Theft

All of the cases discussed above are examples of identity theft on a more or less small scale. Certainly in some of the cases, huge amounts of money were stolen and in almost all of the cases many people were impacted in very significant and negative ways. All of those cases, as important as they may be, pale in comparison with the final case to be discussed, the largest single identity theft case ever uncovered.

In about February 2002, Ford Credit discovered that unauthorized credit reports had been ordered, which triggered an investigation by the FBI and eventually resulted in arrests. Three individuals were eventually charged with violating various federal laws in the commission of a huge case of identity theft. These three individuals and other, unindicted, accomplices were "an identity-theft ring that [by relying] on a low level employee of a Long Island software company[,] stole the credit histories of more than 30,000 people and used them to empty bank accounts and take out false loans, among other crimes, federal authorities in Manhattan said."[23] Phillip Cummings, one of the defendants, was charged with conspiracy to commit wire fraud in violation of Title 18, United States Code, section 1343, which states that

> having devised and intending to devise a scheme and artifice to defraud, and for obtaining money and property by means of false pretenses, representations, and promises, to wit, a scheme to defraud (i) commercial credit history repositories of thousands of consumers' credit reports and (ii) thousands of consumers' personal account information and money, did transmit and cause to be transmitted by means of wire communication in interstate and foreign commerce, writings, signs, signals, pictures and sounds for the purpose of executing such scheme and artifice to (i) Equifax's toll-free 800 telephone lines in Alpharetta, Georgia (ii) TransUnion's toll-free 800 telephone lines in Chicago, Illinois, and (iii) Experian's toll-free 800 telephone lines, through which more than 30,000 credit histories of consumers were unlawfully obtained and millions of dollars in losses were caused.[24]

Linus Baptiste and Hakeem Mohammed, the other two arrested, were also charged in the identity theft scheme with violating the same federal law.[25] "James B. Comey, the United States attorney in Manhattan, said the fraud was 'every American's worst nightmare multiplied tens of thousands of times.' Mr. Comey said that there were likely victims in every state."[26]

The scope and scale of this massive alleged case of identity theft is unprecedented, and illustrates well several points discussed in this book. It certainly raises question about how the law can or should be used to combat a scenario like the one described above. Obviously the answer depends on a number of factors. How any case of identity theft is handled under the law will depend on the jurisdictions involved. In which state or states did the crimes occur? Those states in which crimes occurred have jurisdiction, and the federal government will have jurisdiction when interstate crimes are committed (which is quite common in today's identity theft fact patterns). So there could be overlapping jurisdiction. What jurisdiction should prosecute?—again a difficult

Questions of jurisdiction are often difficult for the legal system to address and those questions are often complicated in identity theft prosecutions. Many issues, both legal and extralegal, must be considered when thinking about jurisdictional questions. The process must be fair but it must also respect the desire for victims and society to have their needs met by the justice system. Below are some questions that arise when thinking about jurisdiction, particularly in cases of identity theft or identity fraud.

Procedural Fairness v. Victims rights: Where would it be fair to proceed with the trial? Where the victim resides? Where the defendant resides? Each option imposes hardships on at least one of the parties.

Federal v. State Jurisdiction: Should criminal charges be filed in federal or state court? If the alleged crime impacted many victims in many states, where should charges be filed? Which jurisdiction should get the first chance to prosecute? Federal and state laws provide different powers and different possible penalties.

Resources: Which agency has the most resources to pursue prosecution? Should government resources impact where a prosecution should occur? Which jurisdiction has the most favorable laws to the fact pattern? The federal government has more resources devoted to identity theft investigation and prosecution but there are questions of state power involved as well.

question, and the answer depends in part on the size and scale of the crime. Different states have widely varying statutes on identity theft. The bigger the crime, the more victims, and the more money involved, the more likely it is that the federal government will prosecute the alleged crimes, as in the case mentioned above.

Which law will prosecutors use to charge the alleged perpetrators of identity theft? Again, the answer depends on the particular fact pattern. Generally, prosecutors will charge the crime as most specifically defined in the statutes. If the actions allegedly committed by the defendant fit the basic elements of multiple crimes, the prosecutor will use his or her discretion to charge the crime under the statute that in his or her judgment best fits the alleged crime. Factors the prosecutor would consider include the severity or maliciousness of the defendant's actions, the evidence against the defendant, and the range of penalties possible under the particular statute charged. In the massive alleged case of identity fraud in New York, the prosecutor chose to charge the defendants under the federal wire fraud statutes, presumably because the evidence was strong, the facts fit the elements of the crime, and the range of punishment available would serve justice in that particular case.

Conclusion

As we have seen, identity theft or identity fraud takes many forms and shapes and is used by many to further a vast array of criminal activities, from international terrorism to bank fraud. Identity fraud was a key step in Ahmed Ressam's plan to infiltrate the United States in an attempt to commit an act of international terrorism. Various forms of identity theft were committed by criminals in California, Florida, and Washington State, in order to further criminal frauds involving large sums of money. And in the Adelaide Andrews case, we learned that employees in places like doctor's offices can sometimes steal sensitive personal information and use it to commit identity theft. Identity theft fact patterns vary widely are often complicated and ancillary to other criminal activity, such as terrorism and bank and other frauds.

There never ceases to be surprising cases of identity theft: A college student recently applied for her first credit card only to find out that she already had more than $50,000 in debt! She was troubled to discover that she was a victim of identity theft, but the worst part was that the thief was her own father![27] The New York case involving one of the largest alleged schemes of identity theft, with more than 30,000 possible victims, illustrates the vast potential harm that perpetrators can cause. It also illustrates the complexity of the law and decisions that prosecutors must make. Identity theft can be perpetrated in a number of creative ways, have a wide range of victims, and can be prosecuted under a wide variety of laws, depending on the circumstances of each particular case.

Conclusions

The scope of the problem of identity theft is tremendous, and it is only increasing. As demonstrated by the previous chapters, identity theft, like most crime, has a significant local impact. That is to say that the crime is committed in local communities in the United States and real individuals at that level can suffer enormous personal and financial consequences. One of the most important characteristics that separates identity theft from other types of crimes is that it frequently does not remain local. The crime of identity theft can be a frightening national level, transborder, or international crime. Unlike street crimes or other local criminal activities, the Internet and technology allow criminals to commit the crime of identity theft against victims literally anywhere in the world.

As our society and the global society continue to grow and advance, problems of identity and identity theft have become and will continue to be more pronounced. We can no longer live in a world where identification is a matter of personal recognition of one another. Nonpersonal identifiers increasingly define identification and identity. These identifiers, precisely because they are random, lacking any meaningful connection to the individual, ironically have had the effect of making identity less rather than more secure. The system that exists now was created in a very different time and for a much more limited purpose. Once the defining characteristics of identity are alienated to government or businesses, we have lost control of those identifiers. With the control goes security.

As we have seen, it may be possible to reverse this trend in the future through yet more technological advances. Ideally a universally secure efficient means of identification (USEMI) can be developed and employed. Whether it can be done in a practical way and quickly enough to thwart the next advances on the part of the thieves remains to be seen. The technology that exists today is certainly far from sufficient to do so. Also problems of cost, convenience, and cultural resistance to more secure means of identification will need to be overcome. While we are all looking for more security in our daily interactions with the system, it is unclear how much convenience we are willing to surrender.

Lacking a USEMI and unable for the moment to stop the tide of identity theft, we are left to pick up the pieces of the lives that are impacted and destroyed through identity theft. Identity theft has enormous costs both in real dollars and in other, human and nonmonetary ways. A victim of identity theft will typically spend hundreds of hours trying to clear his or her name and credit history. The monetary costs to avoid paying the fraudulent credit lines average nearly one thousand dollars and the process takes an average of nearly two years to complete. Above and beyond the cost to the individual victims, the costs to society of dealing with the deluge of new cases are growing rapidly.

Federal and state governments as well as private companies are bearing much of the cost of identity theft. That means that we are all bearing the costs, monetary and otherwise. We all pay through higher costs for goods and services, higher insurance costs, and diversion of taxes away from other causes and toward this fight. Prevention of identity theft is a far better option for individuals and the government than dealing with the aftermath of the damage created by identity thieves. We all need to work for the prevention of identity theft, especially as the problem grows.

In the absence of a systemic solution, the prevention of identity theft becomes a very personal matter. Several steps can be taken to protect against it. Protecting sensitive personal information is the goal, and there are many ways to move toward it. Rent a post office box and drop mail off at the post office, rather than use a home or apartment mailbox. Identity thieves often steal mail from home and apartment mailboxes and by this means obtain information necessary to steal identity.

Obtain and use a good crosscut shredder which cuts documents both vertically and horizontally, reducing them to shreds. Shredders that shred the document into only vertical strips are cheaper but less effective. A determined individual could re-create the document from vertically shredded paper. As we have seen, even a small amount of information disposed of improperly can be the beginning of the road for a committed identity thief. Take garbage directly to the disposal site yourself or put the garbage out just prior to collection to minimize the time a thief would have to search garbage.

Do not use your Social Security number for identification purposes except as required by law. Many of the requests for that most important of identifiers are not covered under the law and can be legally refused. Certainly do not carry your Social Security card in your wallet or purse. When making purchases, use cash when possible to minimize the opportunities for identity thieves to acquire credit information. Reduce the number of credit cards you use and carry or even eliminate them if possible. Be careful about using credit cards if you choose to use them. Think about the business you are dealing with and whether they will keep your information private. Usually if a credit card is used, that information is recorded and stored in store computers, systems that are far from secure against attack by hackers or thieves. The fewer credit cards that are used, the less businesses will know about you. And if they do not have your personal information in their computers, employees and others cannot steal your personal information from that source.

Automatic teller machine (ATM) cards should be treated as credit cards, and checks are vulnerable to similar abuse. Cash is the safest way to conduct business transactions. Do not give out any unnecessary personal information over the Internet. If you must use the Internet to conduct business transactions, think twice about the website you are dealing with and the security of the site and transaction. Every time information is transmitted and shared, there is an electronic record that is created that will probably go into a database.

It is important to opt out of as much information sharing as possible. Contacting each bank, credit card company, and business with which you do business can be time consuming but it is a necessary step. Ask these companies, by whatever means they require, to give your personal information maximum protection. Inform them that you do not wish your information to be shared with any in-house or third-party vendors. It is not possible to recover completely the personal information that has already been disseminated, but to limit future distributions.

Check your credit report with the three major credit reporting agencies at least once a year. You may be able to get a free report each year or have to pay a small fee. By checking your credit report each year, you can see which creditors claim that you owe money and you can double-check the record of your payment history. Checking your credit report may be the first notice of identity theft. Your credit report is very important in determining whether future creditors will loan you money. If you have a poor credit report, you may not qualify for a home loan, car loan, or other important credit. So it is important to check your credit report and make sure there are no errors. By following common sense and guarding to whom you disclose sensitive information, you can minimize the chances of becoming a victim of identity theft.

How can you best deal with identity theft if you are already a victim? There are three things you should do. First you should contact each of the three national credit reporting agencies and request that each place a fraud alert on your account. This action puts potential creditors on notice that someone may try to misrepresent you and commit some type of fraud. Potential creditors should then carefully examine whether or not it is you with whom they are dealing. The three major credit reporting agencies are:

Equifax Credit Information Services, Inc.
PO Box 740241, Atlanta, GA 30374–0241
(800) 525-6285

Experian Information Solutions, Inc.
PO Box 9530, Allen, TX 75013
(888) 397-3742

TransUnion
Fraud Victim Assistance Division
PO Box 6790, Fullerton, CA 92634–6790
(800) 680-7289

Next, contact your city or county law enforcement and file a police report regarding the identity theft and fraud. You should also inform your state attorney general's office and make a report to the Federal Trade Commission at (877) 438-4338. Then obtain a copy of the ID Theft Affidavit from the FTC website located at www.consumer.gov/idtheft/affidavit.htm, and complete it. This affidavit is a standardized form with which you can inform all major credit bureaus and most major creditors. It eliminates a large amount of paperwork (having to complete a different form for each organization). You should send a copy of the completed form to each of the major credit bureaus and to each of your creditors and bank. Visa and MasterCard limit an identity theft victim's liability to $50. It is best to report identity theft as soon as it is discovered—you will be afforded the most protections then, and law enforcement may have a better chance of apprehending the responsible offender(s).

If you know or find out who committed the identity theft, you might have a civil lawsuit option to recover your losses. Oftentimes those who commit identity theft lack significant assets, but over time that can change. You should consult an attorney to see if it makes sense to pursue civil legal action against the offender, or anyone else. Nothing in this book should be construed as legal advice, as nothing here is intended to substitute for consultation with a lawyer. Track your time spent cleaning up the mess created by the identity theft. Keep a day planner and record each phone call in connection with your recovery, to whom made, and duration. Record time spent filling out forms and composing letters, etcetera. Making a record of your recovery activity could help in two specific ways. First, in a criminal sentencing hearing, if the judge is able to consider an exceptional sentence (giving the offender extra time in jail), you may be able to address the court about the impact this crime had on your life. If you demonstrate that you have spent many hours and much effort trying to repair the damage, it will help the judge make a decision. Second, if you do decide to pursue a civil law suit, these records will help an attorney prove civil damages.

Federal and state legislatures have enacted laws against identity theft in an attempt to battle this growing menace. Advances in technology may one day lead to a USEMI. Until that day, law, technology, and, most importantly, individual diligence will remain the best ways to combat identity theft.

Notes

Chapter 1

1. This is known as "recognition based" identification. While very secure, it quickly becomes impractical in a large society. What Lynn M. LoPuki calls "knowledge based" identification (knowing some secret information such as a mother's maiden name), "token based" identification (having the right document such as a passport or driver's license), and perhaps eventually true "biometric identification" (reliance on difficult to alienate innate characteristics like DNA) become much more practical. For a more detailed discussion, see LoPuki, 2001, "Human Identity and the Identity Theft Problem" *Texas Law Review* (80).

2. For a complete discussion of individuality, privacy and the increasing intrusion by government and others into private spaces, see Jeffrey Rosen's excellent work, *The Unwanted Gaze:*

The Destruction of Privacy in America (New York: Random House, 2000).

3. LoPuki, op. cit.

4. Executive Order 9397 reads in part, "[I]t is desirable in the interest of economy and orderly administration that the Federal Government move towards the use of a single unduplicated numerical identification system of accounts and avoid the unnecessary establishment of additional systems: . . . Hereafter any Federal department, establishment, or agency shall, whenever the head thereof finds it advisable to establish a new system of permanent account numbers pertaining to individual persons, utilize exclusively the Social Security Act account numbers assigned pursuant to Title 26, section 402.502 of the 1940 Supplement to the Code of Federal Regulations. . . . The Social Security Board shall provide for the assignment of an account number to each person who is required by any Federal agency to have such a number but who has not previously been assigned such number by the Board."

5. 42 USC, § 405 expressly exempts state agencies when Social Security numbers are used "in the administration of any tax, general public assistance, driver's license, or motor vehicle registration law within its jurisdiction."

6. 5 USC, § 552 requires that any federal, state, or local government agency that requests your Social Security number (SSN) provide you with four pieces of information: They are required to acknowledge the authority (statutory or executive) that authorizes the solicitation of the information and whether disclosure of such information is mandatory or voluntary; the principal purposes for which the information is intended to be used; the routine uses that may be made of the information; and the effects on you, if any, of not providing all or any part of the requested information. In addition, the act makes it illegal for federal, state, and local government agencies to deny any privileges or benefits to individuals who refuse to provide their Social Security numbers unless that disclosure is required by federal statute (5 USC 522, § 7) or the disclosure is to an agency for use in a record system that required the SSN before 1975. (5 USC 552a provides a grandfather clause for these systems.) In most cases, providing a Social Security number is actually optional, and while it may expedite your request, failure to provide it will not otherwise adversely affect your interaction with the agency.

7. "When Bad Things Happen to Your Good Name." 2000. Senate hearing before the Subcommittee on Technology, Terrorism, and Government Information, S. Hrg. 106-885.

8. Since the 1980s, "data matching" has become the norm for the federal government. Of course prior to the computerization of large amounts of public records, data matching was simply not feasible. Today, people who apply for federal jobs can be checked against and matched with the list of people who have failed to register with Selective Service. People applying for veteran's benefits or welfare payments can be compared and matched with those who have federal tax liens or who have unpaid child support judgments against them. The increasing linkage among different databases and different types of data is an enormous boon to those who would steal identity. Today, access to the right single databank can provide more linked and matched information than could have been obtained from many individual databanks only a few years ago. Certainly, it can provide far more information than was available anywhere prior to the advent of computerized databases.

9. It may seem trivial to mention these innocuous types of identity theft but they are not always as trivial as they appear. In any case, theft by family members and by roommates represent the two largest categories of perpetrators of identity theft. According to FTC data, family members account for 4.9 percent of identity theft perpetrators and roommates account for 1.2 percent. Those figures account only for the 10.7 percent of cases in which the identity of the thief is known. In the remaining 89.3 percent of cases, the identity of the criminal is not known at the time of reporting.

10. See Michael Higgins, 1998, "Identity Thieves," *American Bar Association Journal* (42).

11. Nine new lines of credit represent the practical upper limit even for professional identity thieves. Credit companies will generally not secure a line of credit if more than three inquiries have been made into an individual credit history within a one-month period. Given that there are three major credit reporting agencies in the United States, most organizations will attempt to open three lines of credit reported by each of the three different agencies, creating the practical limit of nine. While the presence of a practical limit may seem comforting, it is important to remember that each line of credit may be for tens of thousands of dollars or more. The total for each individual on these nine lines of credit can run easily into six or seven figures, and that does not take into account other simultaneous deleterious effects of retail credit and check fraud.

Chapter 2

1. "Identity Fraud: Prevalence and Links to Alien Illegal Activities." 2002. Hearing before the Subcommittee on Crime, Terrorism, and Homeland Security and the Subcommittee on Immigration, Border Security, and Claims of the Committee on the Judiciary, U.S. House of Representatives.
2. 18 USC § 1028(a)
3. Federal Trade Commission. 2002. "Identity Theft Complaint Data: Figures and Trends on Identity Theft January 2001–December 2001."
4. "Prepared Statement of the Federal Trade Commission on the Identity Theft Penalty Enhancement Act of 2002." Senate hearing before the Subcommittee on Technology, Terrorism, and Government Information of the Senate Judiciary Committee.
5. Federal Trade Commission. 2003. "National and State Trends in Fraud and Identity Theft January–December 2002."
6. For further discussion, see the General Accounting Office document "Identity Theft: Greater Awareness and Use of Existing Data Are Needed," 2002. Report to the Honorable Sam Johnson, House of Representatives (GAO-02-766).
7. "Identity Fraud: Prevalence and Links to Alien Illegal Activities."
8. Almost every website or government agency that deals with identity theft prevention or correction recommends that affected consumers report the theft to all three major credit reporting agencies. It seems then that an aggregation of the numbers reported by the three agencies should show significant duplication. As they do not share that information even with each other, however, the exact amount of overlap in reports is impossible to determine.
9. It may also be the case that the education efforts of the FTC, the FBI, and others have resulted in a higher percentage of victims being willing to report the crimes against them. As with quantifying the actual number of victims, however, this idea relies on significant unsubstantiated conjecture.
10. "SSA/OIG Statement for the Record: Hearing on Social Security Number Misuse." 2000. Before the Subcommittee on Social Security of the House Ways and Means Committee, U.S. House of Representatives.
11. During the same period, 1998 to 2001, the staffing level at the Social Security Administration hotline increased from 11 to 50 people. Decreasing wait times to report Social Security number misuse or other fraud should correlate positively with increasing reports of the crimes.

12. The FTC reports the following percentages on fraud complaints lodged with the Consumer Sentinel Database for 2001: Identity theft (42%), Internet auctions (10%), Internet services and computer complaints (7%), shop-at-home and catalog offers (6%), advance fee loans and credit protection (5%), prize/sweepstakes/gifts (4%), business opportunities and work at home plans (4%), foreign money offers (4%), magazine and buyers clubs (3%) and telephone pay-per-call/information services (2%).

13. SSA, Office of the Inspector General. 1999. "Management Advisory Report—Analysis of Social Security Number Misuse, Allegations Made to the Social Security Administration's Fraud Hotline" (A-15-99-92019).

14. 18 USC § 1028 (which contains (a)(7), the identity theft statute), § 1029, § 1014, § 1344, 42 USC § 408 and 15 USC § 1644.

15. General Accounting Office. 2002. "Report to Congressional Requesters. Identity Theft: Prevalence and Cost Appear to Be Growing" (GAO-02-363).

16. Postal Inspection Service. "2000 Annual Report of Investigations of the United States Postal Inspection Service."

17. Demographic data and data on geographic distribution of identity theft complainants are not currently integrated between the FTC data clearinghouse and the SSA because of differences in how identity theft is investigated and charged by those agencies. The FTC reports that the most frequently targeted age group is people in their thirties, but that information does not take into account the large amount of Social Security-related theft and fraud that is reported to the SSA but not directly to the FTC database. Thus, while it would be useful, it is not really possible in that case to give any authoritative information about the distribution of the crime of identity theft across those parameters or others, such as how the identifying information was obtained by the thief or the lag time between the thief obtaining the information and the discovery of the crime.

18. These data come from the FTC database and represent calls to that database between November 1999 and September 2001.

19. CALPIRG and Privacy Rights Clearinghouse. 2000. "Nowhere to Turn: Victims Speak Out on Identity Theft." See also General Accounting Office, 2002. GAO-02-363.

20. American Bankers Association. 2000. Deposit Account Fraud Survey.

21. American Bankers Association. 2000. Deposit Account Fraud Survey.

22. General Accounting Office, 2002. GAO-02-363.

23. General Accounting Office. 1998. "Report to Congressional Requesters. Identity Fraud: Information on Prevalence, Cost, and Internet Impact Is Limited" (GAO/GGD-98-100BR).
24. General Accounting Office, 2002. GAO-02-363.
25. American Bankers Association. 2000. Op. cit.
26. General Accounting Office, 2002. GAO-02-363.

Chapter 3

1. The big three agencies are Equifax, Experian (formerly TRW Credit), and TransUnion.
2. Consumers do have some rights under the Fair Credit Reporting Act, but these are limited primarily to the ability to have credit bureaus correct errors. Consumers can have little impact on the large credit agencies because the consumer is not necessarily the customer, making the credit bureaus relatively uninterested in her or her concerns about privacy. Most of what these agencies do takes place in secret, and consumers, beyond their few specific rights, have a nearly impossible time trying to learn more.
3. Of course even that system was far from perfect. Information even under Fair Credit Reporting Act standards found its way into the hands of thieves. Under this law, however, the violations were usually relatively small and contained with a single employee of a credit bureau selling information on a few files, for instance. Even if that occurred, it was usually fairly easy to investigate and to track down, arrest, and punish those who violated the law.
4. Most frequently, the big three credit reporting agencies do not sell even header reports directly. In order to shield themselves from possible backlash or legal entanglements, these agencies usually rely on thirdparty brokers to actually sell the information. In many cases, however, these brokers may actually be companies owned by the credit agencies.
5. There are legitimate purposes for these header reports as well. The credit reporting industry lobbied heavily in favor of reducing the protection given this category of information. The industry saw a large market for header information among bail bond agents and private investigation firms.
6. The Gramm-Leach-Bliley Act of 1999 requires that banks do this. An amendment to the law, the Sarbanes amendment, recognized at least implicitly that this may not be sufficient and affirmatively provides states with the ability to enact more exacting protections of consumer control over information sharing. California

has been considering a state law to require an opt-in provision for any third-party information sharing by banks.

7. Steve Blackledge. 2002. *Privacy Denied: A Survey of Bank Privacy Policies*. California Public Interest Research Group: Sacramento.

8. Federal Trade Commission. 2001. *Prepared Statement of the Federal Trade Commission on "Internet Fraud."* The Subcommittee on Commerce, Trade, and Consumer Protection of the Committee on Energy and Commerce of the U.S. House of Representatives.

9. This is a practice known as pretexting and was made specifically illegal under the Gramm-Leach-Bliley Act. Brokers or others engaged in this activity use publicly available information to, for instance, call a bank and convince the bank employee that they are a real person who has an account there. Once they have convinced the bank of their alternate identity, they are able to access secure financial information such as account numbers and balances. The FTC has taken criminal action against many brokers engaging in pretexting after reviewing web-based ads for brokers and finding more than 200 firms that were willing to engage in the practice.

10. Federal Trade Commission. 2001. *Prepared Statement "Internet Fraud."* The Subcommittee on Commerce, Trade and Consumer Protection of the Committee on Energy and Commerce of the United States House of Representatives. Washington, DC.

11. For a more comprehensive overview of the problem of crime on the Internet, see the 2002 report prepared by the National White Collar Crime Center and the Federal Bureau of Investigation, "IFCC 2001 Internet Fraud Report: January 1, 2001–December 31, 2001."

12. General Accounting Office. 2002. Document, "Identity Fraud: Prevalence and Links to Alien Illegal Activities." Testimony before the Subcommittee on Crime, Terrorism, and Homeland Security and the Subcommittee on Immigration, Border Security, and Claims, Committee on the Judiciary, House of Representatives (GAO-02-830T).

13. See "Statement for the Record of Dennis M. Lormel, Chief, Terrorist Financial Review Group, Federal Bureau of Investigation," before the Senate Judiciary Committee Subcommittee on Technology, Terrorism, and Government Information July, 2002.

14. "Credit card theft: Trading virgin ccdz," Joellen Perry, usnews.com, August 28, 2000.

15. "Credit Card Theft Thrives Online as Global Market," Matt Richtel, *The New York Times* on the Web, May 13, 2002.

16. "Two arrested in Wales for credit card theft costing $3 million," staff reports, cnn.com, March 24, 2000. www.nytimes.com.

17. General Accounting Office, GAO-02-830T.
18. In 1998, the Immigration and Naturalization Service (INS) seized more than 24,000 counterfeit Social Security cards in Los Angeles after undercover agents had purchased 10,000 counterfeit permanent resident identification cards (green cards) from a document counterfeiting ring producing them on a large scale. INS data show that from 1999 to the present, the INS has confiscated more than 100,000 false or counterfeit identity documents each year at border crossings.
19. While these technologies have made rapid progress in recent years, they are still far from perfect. The largest producer of this software reports a success rate of 99.32 percent or an error rate of .68 percent. While that is a very small percentage error, in real terms the number of false-positive results from such a system, when it is applied to millions of people, is enormous.
20. This illustrates the problem of systems that are "brittle" or that "break badly." The linking of more and more to any identifier, no matter how secure it appears will only increase, not reduce, the problem. What is needed is either complete security, which is probably not possible, or increased flexibility in the system of identification. For a far more complete discussion, see Bruce Schneier, *Secrets and Lies: Digital Security in a Networked World*. New York: John Wiley, 2000.
21. A Japanese cryptographer working at Yokohoma National University has recently shown that this is entirely possible. Using less that $10 worth of readily available materials, he created artificial thumbprints, gummi-thumbs. These fakes were able to fool eleven of the best fingerprint recognition systems currently available as much as 80 percent of the time. If a professional mathematician could accomplish this, it seems likely that a professional thief would be able to master the technology as well.

Chapter 4

1. These statutes include, but are not necessarily limited to: the 1974 Privacy Act (5 USC Part I, Chapter 5, Subchapter II, § 552); The Truth in Lending Act (15 USC Chapter 41, Subchapter I, Part A, §§ 1601 et seq); The Federal Trade Commission Act (15 USC Chapter 2, Subchapter I, § 45); The Bank Fraud Statute (18 USC Part I, Chapter 63, § 1344); the Social Security Fraud Statute (42 USC Chapter 7, Subchapter II, § 408); the Credit Card Fraud Statute (15 USC Chapter 41, Subchapter I, Part B, § 1644); The Electronic Funds Transfers Act (15 USC Chapter 41, Subchapter VI,

§§ 1693 et seq); the Gramm-Leach-Bliley Act (15 USC Chapter 94, Subchapter I, §§ 6801 et seq); the Racketeer Influenced and Corrupt Organizations Act (RICO), which prohibits racketeering activity and collection of unlawful debt (18 USC Part I, Chapter 96, §§ 1961 et seq); the Wire Fraud Statute (if wire fraud is committed against a financial institution the penalty of imprisonment could be for a period up to 30 years) (18 USC Part I, Chapter 63, § 1343); the Fair Credit Reporting Act (15 USC Chapter 41, Subchapter III, § 1681 et seq); the Fair Credit Billing Act (15 USC Chapter 41, Subchapter I, Part D, §§ 1666 et seq); the Fair Debt Collection Practices Act (15 USC Chapter 41, Subchapter V, §§ 1692 et seq); the Privacy Protection Act of 1980 (42 USC Chapter 21A, Subchapter I, Part A); 15 USC Chapter 41, Subchapter III, §§ 1681 et seq, governs credit reporting agencies.

2. 5 USC Part I, Chapter 5, Subchapter II, § 552 (2000).

3. See the Gramm-Leach-Bliley Act, Public Law 106-102, codified at 15 USC Chapter 94, Subchapter I, §§ 6801–6810 (2000).

4. Ibid., § 501(b).

5. Ibid., § 502(b).

6. Steve Blackledge, CALPIRG. 2002. Privacy Denied: A Survey of Bank Privacy Policies. This report also notes that 41 percent of the consumers surveyed could not recall receiving a privacy or opt-out notice from their bank and 22 percent reported receiving a notice but not reading it.

7. For a complete list of the exceptions to the notice requirement and applicability, one should consult the complete text of sections 502 and 503, respectively; see also 15 USC Chapter 94, Subchapter I, Section 6802.

8. Failure to provide customers with an opt-out notice and information about the information sharing undertaken by the bank would cause the bank to lose its information sharing privileges. While the law creates some substantial new rights, the so-called Sarbanes amendment recognizes that these may not be sufficient to protect privacy. This amendment affirmatively gives to states the power to create even more restrictive financial privacy laws. States such as California have been debating changing the opt-out policy of the federal law to an opt-in policy at the state level, requiring consumers to act affirmatively to allow their information to be shared among financial institutions.

9. 15 USC Chapter 94, Subchapter II, Section 6821(c).

10. Public Law 106-102, Sec. 523, codified at 15 USC Chapter 94, Subchapter II, Section 6823(2000).

11. Cong. Rec. H9996 (1998).

12. Cong. Rec. H9996 (1998).

13. Cong. Rec. S12604 (1998).
14. 18 USC, Part I, Chapter 47, §1028.
15. The Internet False Identification Prevention Act of 2000 became Public Law 106-578, codified at 18 USC Part I, Chapter 47, §1028 (2001).
16. Cong. Rec. S11428-S11429 (2000).
17. 18 USC, Part I, Chapter 47, §§ 1028 et seq. (2000).
18. "Prepared Statement of the Federal Trade Commission on Identity Theft: The Impact on Seniors." before the Senate Special Committee on Aging, July 18, 2002.
19. Press release, United States Sentencing Commission, "Sentencing Commission Toughens Penalties Against Internet Pirates and Sexual Predators Targeting Children, Agency Also Increases Sentences for Methamphetamine Offenses, Identity Theft, and Phone Cloning." April 4, 2000. The amendments took effect November 1, 2000.
20. United States Sentencing Commission. 1999. "Identity Theft Final Report."
21. 15 USC Chapter 41, Subchapter I, Part A, §§ 1601 et seq.
22. 15 USC Chapter 41, Subchapter I, part D, § 1666 (2000).
23. 15 USC Chapter 41, Subchapter I, part B, § 1640 (2000).
24. 15 USC Chapter 41, Subchapter I, part B, § 1635 (2000).
25. 15 USC Chapter 2, Subchapter I, § 45 (2000).
26. 15 USC Chapter 2, Subchapter I, § 45 (a)(1) (2000).
27. 18 USC Part I, Chapter 47 § 1029 deals specifically with "fraud and related activity in connection with access devices."
28. 18 USC Part I, Chapter 47, § 1029.
29. 42 USC Chapter 7, Subchapter II, § 408 (2000).
30. 107th Congress, Senate Bill 848.
31. 18 USC Part I, Chapter 47, § 1031 (2000).
32. 15 USC Chapter 41, Subchapter VI, Section 1693.
33. 15 USC Chapter 41, Subchapter VI, § 1693(g) (2000).
34. 15 USC Chapter 41, Subchapter VI, § 1693 (n) and (m) (2000).
35. 15 USC Chapter 41, Subchapter VI, Section 1693n(6).
36. See *Black's Law Dictionary*, seventh edition, St. Paul, Minn: West Group, 1999, p. 305.
37. 328 US 640 (1946).
38. Some states, like Washington, require that a "substantial step" be taken in furtherance of the conspiracy. See Wash. Rev Code Title 9A.28.040 (2002).
39. See S.1742, 107th Congress, Sponsored by Senator Cantwell, and S.AMDT. 4954 to S. 1742 which was agreed to by Unanimous Consent of the Senate. See also CR S11053–11055, 107th Congress, 2002.

40. Press release, Senator Maria Cantwell, January 22, 2003.

41. S.1702, 107th Congress, 2002.

42. S.1702, 107th Congress, 2002.

43. Press Release, Cantwell, January 22, 2003.

Chapter 5

1. General Accounting Office. 2002. "Identity Theft: Greater Awareness and Use of Existing Data Are Needed." Report to the Honorable Sam Johnson, House of Representatives (GAO-02-766).

2. Many of these state statutes provide threshold levels of theft for these crimes to be charged as felonies. Under the specified thresholds, the crimes would be charged as misdemeanors under these laws.

3. Identity Theft Data Clearinghouse, Federal Trade Commission. 2002. Identity Theft Victims Top 10 Locations (Per 100,000) January 1–December 31, 2001. Figure 5b.

4. Cal. Penal Code, § 530.5 (2002).

5. Cal. Penal Code, § 528 (2002).

6. Cal. Penal Code, § 530.5 (2002).

7. See GAO-02-766. Also General Accounting Office, 2002, "Report to Congressional Requesters. Identity Theft: Prevalence and Cost Appear to be Growing" (GAO-02-363).

8. See for example Beth Givens' testimony before the U.S. Senate on July 12, 2000, *Identity Theft: How it Happens, Its Impact on Victims and Legislative Solutions.* Written Testimony prepared for U.S. Senate Judiciary Subcommittee on Technology, Terrorism and Government Information, John Kyl, Chairman.

9. Cal. Penal Code, § 530.6 (2002).

10. Cal. Penal Code, § 530.6 (2002).

11. Fla. Stat, Title XLVI, Chapter 817, Part I, §§ 817.568 et seq. (2002).

12. Fla. Stat, Title XLVI, Chapter 817, Part I, §§ 817.568 2(a) and 2(b). (2002).

13. Fla. Stat, Title XLVI, Chapter 817, Part I, § (4) (2002).

14. Fla. Stat, Title XLVI, Chapter 817, Part I, § (6)(a) (2002).

15. Ill. Comp Stat, Ch 720 5/Article 16G et seq (2002).

16. Ill. Comp Stat, Ch 720 5/Article 16G-15(d)(1)-(5) (2002).

17. Ill. Comp Stat, Ch 720 5/Article 16-G5 (2002).

18. Ill. Comp Stat, Ch 720 5/Article 16G-20 (2002).

19. Ill. Comp Stat, Ch 720 5/Article 16G-20(e) (2002).

20. Wash. Rev Code, Title 9.35.020(2)(a) and (b) (2002).

21. Wash. Rev Code, Title 9A.20.21(c) (2002).

22. Wash. Rev Code, Title 9A.20.21(b) (2002).
23. Wash. Rev Code, Title 9A.20.21(a) (2002).
24. Wash. Rev Code, Title 9.35.001 (2002).
25. Wash. Rev Code, Title 9.35.020(1) (2002).
26. Wash. Rev Code, Title 9.35.010(6) (2002).
27. Wash. Rev Code, Title 9.35.020(4) (2002).
28. Wash. Rev Code, Title 9.35.020(5) (2002).
29. Wash. Rev Code, Title 9.35.040 (2002).
30. Wash. Rev Code, Title 9.35.800 (2002).
31. Wash. Rev Code, Title 19.182.160 (2002).
32. *State v. Baldwin,* 111 Wn. App. 631 (2002).
33. *State v. Baldwin,* 111 Wn. App. 631, 635–637 (2002).
34. *State v. Baldwin,* 111 Wn. App. 631, 638 (2002).
35. *State v. Baldwin,* 111 Wn. App. 631, 649 (2002).

Chapter 6

1. "Identity Theft: Greater Awareness and Use of Existing Data Are Needed." Report to the Honorable Sam Johnson, House of Representatives (GAO-02-766) pp. 1–2, 9.
2. Ibid., p. 11.
3. Information in the case of Ahmed Ressam and Mokhtar Haouari is drawn from the transcript of proceedings pages 505–585, United States District Court Southern District of New York, United States of America v. Mokhtar Haouari, Defendant. July 3, 2001; excerpts of this same testimony can be viewed on *Frontline*'s website at www.pbs.org, "Trail of a Terrorist." For more information, see also *The Terrorist Within: The Story Behind One Man's Holy War Against America,* the *Seattle Times,* a special report by Hal Berton, Mike Carter, David Heath, and James Neff, June 23–July 7, 2002.
4. Statement of Attorney General John Ashcroft on conviction of Ahmed Ressam, 152 04-06-01, April 6, 2001.
5. CNN.com/Law Center, "Y2K bomb plotter still talking; sentence delayed," April 1, 2002.
6. Tom Hays, Associated Press, as carried by the *Detroit News,* "Man gets maximum sentence in bomb plot," January 17, 2002.
7. United States of America v. Mokhtar Haouari, op. cit., 538.
8. Ibid, 551.
9. Complaint against Ahmed Ressam, United States of America, Plaintiff, v. Ahmed Ressam, Defendant. Magistrate's docket No. 99-547M, Count II, paragraphs 2 and 3.
10. Press release, Alejandro N. Mayorkas, United States Attorney, Central District of California, July 13, 2000.

11. Press release, Mayorkas, January 10, 2000.
12. Press release, United States Attorney, Eastern District of California, May 18, 2000.
13. Press release, Guy A. Lewis, United States Attorney, Southern District of Florida, and Frank Estrada, Special Agent in Charge, United States Secret Service, 2001.
14. Press release, Lewis and Jose Marrero, Special Agent in Charge, Criminal Investigation Division, Internal Revenue Service, South Florida District, 2001.
15. Press release, Lewis and Frank Estrada, Special Agent in Charge, Miami Field Office, United States Secret Service, and Arthur L. Kuhn, Acting Special Agent in Charge, Orlando Field Office, United States Secret Service, April 19, 2001.
16. Press release, Katrina C. Pflaumer, United States Attorney, Western District of Washington, and Carmen Keller, Regional Commissioner, Social Security Administration, April 25, 2000.
17. Ibid.
18. Press release, Pflaumer, April 13, 2001.
19. Press release, Pflaumer and Robert Morgan, Postal Inspector in Charge, U.S. Postal Inspection Service, March 9, 2001.
20. *TRW Inc. v. Andrews*, 534 U.S. 19 (2001); see also *Andrews v. TRW Inc.*, 225 F.3d 1063 (9th Cir.2000).
21. *TRW Inc. v. Andrews*.
22. For a more complete discussion of theories of liabilities for financial institutions, see, "Financial Institutions' Duty of Confidentiality to Keep Customer's Information Secure from the Threat of Identity Theft." 34 U.C. Davis L.Rev. 1077 (2001).
23. "Identity Ring Said To Victimize 30,000." Benjamin Weiser, *New York Times,* p. 1, continued A25, November 26, 2002.
24. Complaint, United States of America v. Phillip Cummings, Defendant. Southern District of New York, November 22, 2002. (Obtained from findlaw.com)
25. Complaint, United States of America v. Linus Baptiste, Defendant. Southern District of New York, c. October 29, 2002. (Obtained from findlaw.com) Indictment, United States of America v. Hakeem Mohammed, Defendant. Southern District of New York, after July, 2002. (Obtained from findlaw.com)
26. Weiser, *New York Times*.
27. "When the identity thief is your dad," msnbc.com/news, November 28, 2002.

GENERAL EDITORS
David A. Schultz & Christina DeJong

Studies in Crime and Punishment is a multidisciplinary series that publishes scholarly and teaching materials from a wide range of methodological perspectives and explores sentencing and criminology issues from a single nation or comparative perspective. Subject areas to be addressed in this series include, but will not be limited to: criminology, sentencing and incarceration, policing, law and the courts, juvenile crime, alternative sentencing methods, and criminological research methods.

For additional information about this series or for the submission of manuscripts, please contact:

David A. Schultz
Peter Lang Publishing
Acquisitions Department
275 Seventh Avenue, 28th floor
New York, New York 10001

To order other books in this series, please contact our Customer Service Department:

(800) 770-LANG (within the U.S.)
(212) 647-7706 (outside the U.S.)
(212) 647-7707 FAX

Or browse online by series:

www.peterlangusa.com